THE INFLUENTIAL LEADER

JOHN EDMUND HAGGAI

HARVEST HOUSE PUBLISHERS

EUGENE, OREGON

Cover by Abris, Veneta, Oregon

Cover photo © Soubrette / iStockphoto

THE INFLUENTIAL LEADER
Copyright © 2009 by John Edmund Haggai
Published by Harvest House Publishers
Eugene, Oregon 97402
www.harvesthousepublishers.com

Library of Congress Cataloging-in-Publication Data
Haggai, John Edmund.
[Lead on!]
The influential leader / John Edmund Haggai.
   p. cm.
Originally published: Lead on! Waco, Tex.: Word Books, c1986.
Includes bibliographical references and index.
ISBN 978-0-7369-2628-7 (pbk.)
1. Leadership—Religious aspects—Christianity. I. Title.
BV4597.53.L43H34 2009
253—dc22

                                                        2008049433

Printed in the United States of America

          09 10 11 12 13 14 15 16 17 / DP-NI / 10 9 8 7 6 5 4 3 2 1

To the memory of
Dr. Han Kyung Chik of Korea,
Justice Lai Kew Chai of Singapore, and
Cecil B. Day of Atlanta, Georgia, USA

CONTENTS

PREFACE

I have circled the world more than a hundred times. For 60 years, I have been observing leaders from Asia, Africa, Latin America, and Oceania. I have been with heads of state and heads of corporations and international bankers. I have made it my quest to study top leaders and determine what makes them great.

The first thing to say about leadership is this: Leadership frequently gets mistaken for other things. "Too often, attempts to analyze leadership tend to fail because the would-be analyst misconceives his task. He usually does not study leadership at all. Instead, he studies popularity, power, showmanship, or wisdom in long-range planning."[1]

So said the celebrated psychologist W.C.H. Prentice, writing for the *Harvard Business Review*. Prentice was right. To his list of mistaken definitions of leadership, I could add many more: organizational acumen, administrative expertise, and sheer hard work. All of these are important. But none addresses the subject of leadership.

I believe that leadership consists of *decisions*. Influential leadership, by which I mean broadly leadership that changes the world for the good, consists of decisions, big and small, that derive their inspiration and direction from a single life aim.

For many years now, Haggai Institute has been providing advanced leadership training to highly positioned leaders from the developing world. Men and women who are already great leaders come to Haggai Institute to hone and sharpen their leadership skills.

Among the multiple tens of thousands of people who have been through this training are leading statesmen, authors, generals, university presidents, architects, lawyers, archbishops, celebrated doctors, media moguls, and many others. Influential leaders exist in every culture and profession. And they all demonstrate a propensity to make what in this book I refer to as "visionary decisions."

Leadership also transcends cultures—in spite of the enormous cultural differences that separate the peoples of the earth. And yet influential leadership is a constant, like the law of gravity. Drop a stone in Beijing, and it will fall to the ground just as surely as it does in New York. So it is with the power of visionary decision making.

Leadership also transcends all forms of organization. People talk about "business leadership" and "political leadership" and "military leadership." Yet the fundamentals underlying good leadership have nothing to do with the specifics of business or politics or warfare. Being a discipline in itself, leadership applies with equal effectiveness to any organization and any purpose.

For that reason, I have drawn examples from a range of areas. Many of the people I discuss are business leaders. Others are leaders of nations, leaders of movements, leaders of universities, leaders of communities. All are relevant. In particular, I have made a close study of the leadership shown by Jesus Christ, who qualifies as simply the greatest leader who ever lived.

The ideas in this book are important not only for those who lead big corporations, but for those who lead small organizations as well. Many people reading this book will exercise their leadership in a local neighborhood group or church. Many more, who work in larger corporations, will also occupy leadership positions in groups outside the workplace. Almost all will have some kind of leadership role among friends and family.

This book aims to demystify leadership practice in every area. It aims to encourage potential leaders to overcome their fear of risk. It aims to help you rise to your full potential.

I hope you will read the following pages carefully, then read them again, then write notes all over them to help you internalize and apply the ideas they contain.

These twelve chapters outline major visionary decisions—decisive steps that you can take to move toward being an influential leader. They are not sequential steps; you do not have to become a persuasive communicator *before* you can profit from impossible setbacks. But every step, in every area, will help ignite the kind of thinking and the kind of action that characterizes the world's great leaders.

Leadership is an awesome responsibility and a God-given privilege. I hope and pray that, through reading this book, your leadership will become, not just competent, but truly influential.

John Edmund Haggai
Atlanta, Georgia, U.S.A.

ACKNOWLEDGMENTS

The inspiration for this book began with my parents. My father's example in leadership I refer to in the first chapter. I must also mention my mother, whose ability to communicate with people of all ages, echelons, and cultures still guides my thinking and, I hope, my relationships. She steered me toward great reading and writing. Not once did she belittle my dreams.

Besides my parents, I can name a host of others whose contribution to my life and understanding has influenced this volume—only some of whom I have space to acknowledge here.

Tom Haggai, my brother, with whom I have interacted for more than 50 years on the subject of leadership.

Three missionaries, all deceased, who made a profound impact on my early days, from four years of age to eighteen years of age: Paul Metzler, Carl Tanis, and Paul Fleming.

Ernest H. Watson of Australia, of whom you will read in this book. Sir Cyril Black of Wimbledon, England.

Paul M. Cell, who first opened my eyes to the importance and teaching of the stewardship of money.

Two speech professors who taught me communications: Professor J. Manley Phelps of DePaul University and T.J. Bittikofer of Moody Bible Institute.

Matthijs Van den Heuvel of the Netherlands, Portugal, and now Switzerland, who, in the 1960s and 1970s, demonstrated a leadership in Portugal that God used to bring blessings of beneficial permanence to thousands of Portuguese, both Catholics and Protestants.

J.C. Massee, who influenced my life from 1938 until he passed away at the age of 94.

Paul J. Meyer, progenitor of Success Motivation Institute of Waco, Texas. Leaders in 75 nations concur he has produced the best motivation materials available. I recommend them without reservation.

Dr. Anthony D'Souza of the Xavier Institute of Leadership in Mumbai (Bombay) and faculty member of Haggai Institute.

Michael Youssef, much of whose Ph.D. work focused on the father of contemporary leadership studies, Max Weber of Germany.

Dr. Benjamin Moraes of Brazil.

Bishop Chandu Ray of Pakistan and Australia.

Dr. George Samuel of India.

The men and women who have served on the various Haggai Institute boards of directors and trustees around the world.

Larry Stone, whose superb editing and counsel brought an earlier volume on leadership to a final conclusion and publication—and thus impacted this book.

Norma Byrd, my research and literary assistant, whose expertise in checking out syntax, grammar, and structure made for greater clarity.

Dr. Won Sul Lee of Korea, who urged me for ten years to write a book on leadership.

David Lee, my literary alter ego.

Finally I want to give special thanks to my wife, Christine, for patiently enduring my long stretches of preoccupation during the writing of the book. Her influence, in ministry as well as the home, has been extensive.

THE INFLUENTIAL LEADER

I remember vividly the day I stole my dad's car.

I was 13. My father, a clergyman, had walked to choir practice about two miles away. That meant the car was free.

Going into his closet, I took out the suit he had been wearing that day, pulled the trousers off the hanger, grabbed them by the cuffs, and shook them vigorously. With a *clink* the keys hit the floor.

I told my brother Ted, who was about 12, that I planned to take the car for a spin. I knew he'd refuse to come. I had no passion for Ted's company, but I knew that making him a conspirator was the best way to keep him quiet.

I drove my father's car—a distinctive black 1932 Oldsmobile sedan with yellow spoke wheels—to the top of Power Brothers Hill outside Brockton, Massachusetts, and then jammed the accelerator to the floor.

I was probably doing 70 miles an hour when I roared past another vehicle coming the other direction. I didn't know it then, but the other vehicle contained a member of the choir—and my grandfather.

When my grandfather reached the choir practice, he was dumbfounded to see my father already there.

"Waddy," he said, "how could you get her so soon? I just saw you driving lickety-split toward Brockton!"

That did it. In about an hour my brother Ted arrived with the breaking news. "Dad and all the choir members know that you were driving the car!"

It was a Friday night. I retired hastily to my room. For some reason I had no desire to get up on Saturday morning and face the music. My father, a disciplinarian of the old school, never hesitated to administer punitive action in the wake of disobedience.

I stayed in bed until I could stand the hunger pains no longer. At about ten o'clock I walked downstairs. Dad was sitting in his rocking chair, reading.

Dad never said a word to me about the episode.
He never brought it up.

"Good morning, Son," he said.

I responded quietly, "Hi, Dad."

I briefly scanned his face for some evidence of impending doom, but found none. In fact, Dad never said a word to me about the episode. He never brought it up.

For six weeks I walked around like an overheated boiler, full of guilt and uncertainty. Finally I couldn't take it any longer. I went to my father and blurted out, "Dad, I'm sorry!"

Looking up, he raised an eyebrow. "Oh? Sorry for what?"

He wasn't going to make this easy. I swallowed hard.

"I'm sorry for breaking the law and violating your trust by taking the car out for a ride."

Silence set in.

Then, to my surprise, Dad put his arm around me and said, "I'm glad you owned up to it, Son."

The look on my face probably alerted him to my most pressing concern—what punishment he would mete out to settle the score.

But Dad only looked me in the eye and added, "I think you have already suffered enough."

I never took the car again. And looking back, Dad's handling of this episode—which must have seemed a minor matter in comparison to the many other pressures he confronted—marked my first glimpse of what real leadership is all about.

Visionary Decisions

Globally, those occupying leadership positions probably number in the hundred millions. But only a minority of them will qualify for the title "influential leaders"—that is, leaders who use their influence to transform the world around them and leave a lasting impact for good.

What sets apart influential leaders?

It's easy to rattle off a few highly respected names—George Washington, Benjamin Franklin, Mahatma Gandhi, Mother Teresa, Nelson Mandela—and conclude that such people are set apart by the times they lived in, by their education, by their high ideals, or simply by being unusually good.

But all that misses the point.

In the last 80 years I have met hundreds of influential leaders. I have observed the advanced training of influential leaders. And I have read the biographies of influential leaders I can no longer reach on the phone. I can say with assurance that not all of these men and women score highly on the scales of sainthood or academic intelligence. Each of them has one dominant characteristic: *a particular way of making decisions.*

The trail of decisions a leader leaves behind him charts the trajectory of his influence.

Decision making sits at the heart of leadership. In fact leadership really boils down to a constant execution of decisions, big and small, day in, day out. And the trail of decisions a leader leaves behind him charts the trajectory of his influence.

In my father's case, the trail began with his decision to flee from persecution in Syria and become an American citizen. Throughout his long life, he exerted a powerful influence—by his preaching, by his example, and by stories told worldwide to leaders who never met him. Like all influential leaders, he had a gift for "visionary decision making" that showed itself in everything he did.

Faced with a young joyriding teenager, most parents would wade into a lecture on the evils of irresponsible risk-taking. They would then summarily ground the offender in the belief that swift recompense will make him "think twice before pulling a stunt like that again."

Dad took a different line. He could have bawled me out, or worse; after all, quite apart from the charges of reckless endangerment, I'd broken the law. Instead, he let me stew. And he let me stew for *six weeks* without once letting it affect either his composure or the order of the household.

This was a man who knew clearly where his priorities lay. Almost everything he did was guided by his spiritual commitment. So when eldest son John Edmund rashly put at risk both his own life and the reputation of the pastor's family, Dad sat on his urge to lash out. Instead he chose a course of action that would bring me to recognize, of my own volition, both the magnitude of my error and the need for corrective action.

Visionary decision making makes a direct connection between the here and now and a leader's deepest aims and aspirations.

It worked.

I call this "visionary decision making" because it makes a direct connection between the here and now and a leader's deepest aims and aspirations. It applies to decision making everywhere, from the home to the highest corporate boardroom. It goes beyond simple goal setting.

It denotes a meticulous consistency between daily decisions and your answer to the question: "What is your life ultimately about?"

Amazingly, the multimillion dollar media industry centered on the concept of leadership has almost nothing to say about this. You won't find this issue addressed at most fancy conferences on leadership. Most of the leadership books and magazines on sale at international airports have little if anything to say about it. Yet the shift in values on decision making over the last half century has been seismic.

The Man Who Wouldn't

One quote sums up the philosophy of President Harry S. Truman: "No matter how big a ranch ya' own, or how many cows ya' brand, the size of your funeral is still gonna depend on the weather."

When Truman retired from office in 1952, his income consisted of little more than a U.S. Army pension, reportedly totaling just $13,507.72 per year.

Sometime later, a report came to Congress that Truman was paying for his own stamps and personally licking them. They granted him an allowance and, eventually, an additional pension worth $25,000 per year.

Truman had been offered some lucrative corporate positions, but he declined, stating, "You don't want me. You want the office of the president, and that doesn't belong to me. It belongs to the American people, and it's not for sale."

On May 6, 1971, as Congress prepared to award him the Medal of Honor on his 87th birthday, he refused to accept it. He wrote: "I don't consider that I have done anything which should be the reason for any award, congressional or otherwise."

The fact that most readers will raise their eyebrows at this just shows how low our expectations have sunk. An ex-president who refuses to capitalize on his past position, who refuses a prestigious national award? Why on earth do that?

Truman penned some enduring phrases. Among the best remembered are: "If you can't stand the heat, get out of the kitchen," and "The buck stops here." His advice on winning in politics ("Always be sincere, even if you don't mean it") shows both a survivor's instinct and wry poet's wit.

But beneath the hard-boiled pragmatist one finds a man unable to stray far from his inner convictions. Given the choice between the presidency and world peace, he said once, he would choose world peace every time. The trappings of high office did not impress him. Never once did he lose sight of the fact that his life and career served a higher purpose. He refused the Medal of Honor because he knew he mattered less than the cause he served.

Leaders without vision are like guides without a map.

Truman would not have described this as a vision—but that's what it was. A person with a vision sees the bigger picture. In fact he can never *not* see the bigger picture. And that enables him to take his bearings from it even when those around him see nothing at all.

By contrast, leaders without vision are like guides without a map. Though they may come across as strong, confident, and independent, in reality they are not influencers but influencees. Titles count for nothing. Even as PhDs, chairmen, and CEOs, they blow with the wind of current fashion. Most think short-term or, at most, in a five-year time frame. They respond to situations rather than setting directions. History quickly forgets them.

Tragically, the loss of a compelling vision among leaders has trickled down from the presidency of corporations, the governorship of states, and the pulpits of churches. It corrupts even the leadership of families. The crisis, more pronounced in the West, spreads to many locales across the globe. Couples divorce rather than sort out their problems. Parents focus too much on their own lives and careers and neglect their children. Significantly, parents talk about "managing" children, not about "leading" them.

> *Our world's societies plead for*
> *leadership—in business, in education,*
> *in politics, in the home, in religion.*

At all levels, our world's societies plead for leadership—in business, in education, in politics, in the home, in religion. People know influential leadership when they see it. They mistrust elitists who talk about fairness or compassion but never match their words with action. They grow weary of quick fixes that fail to address the real issues. They see through the blandishments of power-seekers and self-publicists. Instinctively, they seem to know the world needs better leadership than that.

The prophet Ezekiel summed it up when he quoted God as saying, "I sought for a man among them who would make a wall, and stand in the gap before Me on behalf of the land, that I should not destroy it; but I found no one" (Ezekiel 22:30).

But influential leaders haven't disappeared. And if you've met one you'll remember it, because visionary decision making tends to permeate everything he does. So influential leaders will usually have:

- A generous endowment of physical and emotional energy
- A compelling purpose that drives toward a specific goal
- A mastery of the methods for achieving the aim they profess
- An ability to sustain the confidence, loyalty, and frequently the affection of those they lead
- A gift for enlisting followers to support a cause that leads to the followers' own best interests

Tyranny Is Not Leadership

Here someone will object: "But isn't there such a thing as bad influence?"

Yes, plenty of managers in the private and public sectors act like petty dictators. And you don't need much history to know that a person seized with ambition can command the hysterical allegiance of the masses. Influence and vision can both exist on the dark side.

> *To the extent that those in positions*
> *of power neglect their moral*
> *responsibilities, they fail to lead.*

But here's the point. The tyrants, big and small, do not fully deserve the title *leader*. They may rule a department of 200 people. They may rule a political party or an entire nation. But one cannot call them leaders without heavy qualification because power and leadership are not the same thing. To the extent that those in positions of power neglect their moral responsibilities, they fail to lead.

In 1986, after years of thinking, I developed my definition of leadership:

> Leadership is the discipline of deliberately exerting special influence within a group to move it toward goals of beneficial permanence that fulfill the group's real needs.

Every word has been weighed carefully:

Leadership is the discipline…This indicates that leaders are made not born. From time to time a person may intuitively display a leadership characteristic. But that no more makes him a leader than hitting a lucky hole in one makes him a PGA champion. Even these so-called "natural leaders" will not succeed in leadership unless they work hard to perfect themselves. Influential leadership takes discipline.

*...of deliberately exerting...*Leadership takes conscious commitment—a commitment not to the thrill of being respected or obeyed, but to the deeper, spiritual calling of leadership. Only leaders who have this commitment will survive the times of crisis. Influential leaders stick to their task, even when they suffer the most painful reverses. Such commitment does not appear magically out of the air. To develop commitment, a leader will need deep spiritual roots. This explains why many of the greatest business leaders I know begin their board meetings with prayer and keep Bibles on their desks. I have encountered this in Japan and Fiji, in Germany and Lebanon, in Brazil and Canada, in China, on the subcontinent of India, and the great continent of Africa.

*...special influence...*When you exert force on others, they follow you out of fear. By contrast, a leader's authority rests upon a profound trust among his followers. They are convinced that, through him and with him, they can realize self-enriching, humanitarian, and ennobling results they would otherwise fail to attain. They do this because the leader himself displays love, humility, and self-control.

*...within a group...*The group may be a family, a tribe, a company, a church, a neighborhood, a union, or a nation. It may be a loose affiliation of people who share the same interest or passion for sport or educational background. Leaders always exist among, and are operative within, a group of people who share some form of shared identity and shared purpose. Indeed unity of purpose may bring the group into existence and define its goals. Political pressure groups bring together those who feel the same way about an issue, be it the protection of the environment or need for funding of medical research. Companies bring employees together under the shared goal of winning a larger market share.

*...to move it toward goals...*The word *goals* here has two meanings. Broadly, it refers to the leader's vision, his dream of what he sees his group being or doing. The leader's vision sets him apart and makes him a leader, and his commitment to act upon the vision

turns it into a mission. Also, however, *goals* refers to a set of specific, time-sensitive, measurable steps by which a vision and mission can find fulfillment.

*...of beneficial permanence...*A leader's vision should encompass changes that continue and endure for time and eternity. Clearly, such changes can be positive or negative. *Beneficial permanence,* therefore, indicates that true leadership seeks goals that are both lasting and good. Powerholders often seek to achieve goals that benefit themselves or their families or their financial backers—not on the group's behalf but at the group's expense. Such leadership quickly implodes. I find this true even within families. A parent who fails to raise a child with proper wisdom and discipline, for example, will produce results in the child's personality that are permanent but far from beneficial.

...that fulfill the group's real needs. I have written this book for those who desire to develop leadership with the dimension of beneficial permanence. To do this, the leader must have an understanding of the real needs of others. Leaders must maintain a sensitivity, a keen awareness, of the people for whom they have been given responsibility. They are attuned to their surroundings, able to assess situations thoroughly, and prepared to take action. "Fulfilling the group's real needs" is the final test of the genuineness of vision. Such influential leadership demands foresight, wisdom, and determination. In history, nations, movements, and communities have seldom desired things that represent their true best interests.

Abraham Lincoln moved the United States toward goals that fulfilled the real needs of the people—unity with freedom for all citizens—even though many people could not foresee the benefits that would flow from his actions.

For Christians, this definition of leadership has a powerful implication.

If you are a Christian believer in an unbelieving society, *you are a leader.* Let me say that again: To be a Christian in secular society is to be a leader. You may or may not occupy a leadership position in a

Christian organization or the business world. But even if you feel no special calling and hold no position of responsibility, the burden of leading others to salvation falls directly on your shoulders.

Jesus said, "You are the light of the world. A city that is set on a hill cannot be hidden" (Matthew 5:14). He explicitly commanded every believer to put world evangelism in a place of priority. His command applies to all believers in all ages: "Go therefore and make disciples of all the nations, baptizing them in the name of the Father and of the Son and of the Holy Spirit" (Matthew 28:19; see also Mark 16:15 and Acts 1:8).

Christians should not regard world evangelism as a hobby but as an all-consuming priority. There are many ways to carry it out. Evangelism does not just mean being a missionary or pastor. Korean educator Helen Kim, Wall Street investment banker Thomas F. Staley, German-American industrialist John Bolten, leading Brazilian jurist Benjamin Moraes—all these were leaders both in their professional fields and in the mission field.

---

*Christian believers understand
what it means to live for something
greater than themselves.*

When it comes to visionary decision making, Christian believers enjoy an advantage. They understand what it means to live for something greater than themselves. They have internalized the truth that "one's life does not consist in the abundance of the things he possesses" (Luke 12:15).

How to Become a "Born Leader"

I am going to speak openly about my own experience. Many who knew me at the age of 13 still marvel that I ever attained leadership status, leadership performance, and leadership recognition. As I reflect upon my early life, I'm compelled to agree with them that no one demonstrated such an absence of leadership qualities as I.

No one would have considered my looks impressive. I was short. I was sickly. At the age of three, a disease doctors could not identify nearly ended my life. I spent 14 hours a day in bed up until my early teens. Throughout my childhood, life-threatening ailments prophesied an early death. Cholera, smallpox (despite a vaccination that obviously did not take), glandular problems, and a host of other maladies necessitated stays at hospital. I lived on cod-liver oil.

At school, I stuttered and stammered like an arc light in trouble. If I got excited, people around me needed a towel and an umbrella. Not surprisingly, my voice evoked taunting from other children. Even my father, who loved me unconditionally, requested that I tone it down during his time of study. I can still hear the words, "John Edmund, I'm trying to study. Please speak more softly. Your voice pierces me like a knife blade."

As I look back on those episodes I cannot fault him. He had to prepare his sermons. Nevertheless his rebukes did not instill self-confidence.

On top of all that, my congenital shyness drove me up to my bedroom to avoid the embarrassment of meeting visitors to our home. More than once my father threatened punitive action if I did not join the visitors in our living room.

Nevertheless, by age 30 I had served some of America's outstanding congregations as senior minister. At 32, I had addressed 10,000 leaders gathered at Kiel Auditorium in Kansas City, Missouri. The address hit the front pages of America's papers from the *New York Times* to the *Los Angeles Examiner*.

In 1969 I founded a global leadership organization that has provided advanced leadership training to multiple tens of thousands. Its alumni include the world's premier leaders: senior executives, chief justices, university presidents, evangelists, bishops and archbishops, media moguls, political leaders, and parliamentarians.

You can develop leadership capability even if, like me, you appear at first to be hopelessly unpromising leadership material.

The kid who stole his dad's car at age 13 went on to be entertained 18 times in China's Great Hall of the People, and to meet privately with heads of state such as Egypt's President Sadat, Indonesia's President Suharto, and India's Indira Gandhi.

None of which I set down to inflate my own ego, but simply to point out that you can develop leadership capability. You can develop it even if, like me, you appear at first to be hopelessly unpromising leadership material.

In America we refer to some folk as "born leaders." The phrase suggests that some people take naturally to a leadership role because they are born with the characteristics that make for strong leaders. It also suggests that your destiny as a leader or a follower is settled before you have even learned to walk.

Yes, some people have aptitudes that make them develop into good leaders. But the people who are naturally gifted at leadership often do the least to develop those gifts. Consequently, they may fail to fulfill their potential.

Natural gifts alone do not make a leader.

Harvard Business Review collected 15 articles on leadership under the title "Paths Toward Personal Progress: Leaders Are Made, Not Born." These articles explained that natural gifts alone do not make a leader. Indeed, those gifts will never surface if the person does not make the effort to develop and exercise them. Leadership depends upon personal discipline and social environment for ultimate expression and development.[2]

A voice coach once told the young Mary Martin that she should abandon her goal to become a singer. She had an inferior voice, he said, and would never make it in professional music. Mary Martin determined otherwise, and for half a century reigned as one of America's most respected and popular singers. She overcame her aptitude deficiency with exacting self-discipline.

My brother Ted wanted to become an electrical engineer. His college aptitude tests put him at the bottom of the class in math. His teachers told him to forget his chosen field and select another. He refused. Day after day, he worked on developing skill in math. He lost 30 pounds, and his adviser feared for his health. But by his third year in college, Ted was tutoring in math and graduated with honors. Later, he received the L.A. Hyland Award for scientific achievement.

In his youth, the Greek orator Demosthenes suffered such a speech impediment that he was embarrassed to speak to a group. But he resolved to overcome his problem. He shaved one side of his head so he wouldn't be tempted to waste time by seeing anybody. Then he invested agonizing hours in unrelenting practice to overcome his speech problems. Demosthenes became one of the most famous orators of all time.

Summary

The world needs leaders. We are seeing a global crisis of leadership, a crisis brought about by a rapid expansion of world population and by the fact that too many in leadership positions treat leadership as a technical skill, not as a discipline deeply rooted in faith and character.

This book will help you develop into an influential leader. Everyone has the potential to do this because the essence of influential leadership is a certain form of decision making—visionary decision making, meaning decision making driven consistently by the same underlying convictions and life goals.

The following 12 chapters describe 12 steps you can take to achieve influential leadership. Each step requires you to make a visionary decision—that is, a decision that will mark a clear move in the direction of real influence. The first step? Understanding and seizing the vision that drives you.

Leadership is something you do.

Force of habit makes us think of leadership as a state of being. We look at a certain person and we say that he or she is a leader. In reality, the idea of being a leader makes sense only within an organizational structure. The managing director remains the managing director only in the company headquarters; in the taxi going home he's just another man on a commute. That he sits in the managing director's office, attends meetings, and makes phone calls does not in itself confirm his leadership as authentic.

Leadership is something you *do*. History will judge the success or failure of your career, in business or the pastorate, by the quality of the decisions you made. They may be mundane and pragmatic decisions. Or they may be visionary decisions.

It's up to you to decide.

DECIDE TO DEFINE
YOUR VISION

Although President Abraham Lincoln had signed the Emancipation Proclamation in 1863, segregation for blacks lingered on. Exactly a hundred years later, in a famous speech at the Lincoln Memorial, Martin Luther King Jr. expressed his vision for America. He wanted "the riches of freedom and the security of justice" for all people.

> Now is the time to lift our nation from the quicksand of racial injustice to the solid rock of brotherhood. Now is the time to make justice a reality for all of God's children...
>
> I say to you today, my friends, that in spite of the difficulties and frustrations of the moment, I still have a dream...I have a dream that one day on the red hills of Georgia, the sons of former slaves and the sons of former slave owners will be able to sit down together at the table of brotherhood. I have a dream that one day even the state of Mississippi, a state sweltering with the heat of injustice and oppression, will be transformed into an oasis of freedom and justice. I have a dream that my four little children will one day live in a nation where they will not be judged by the color of their skin but by the content of their character. I have a dream...of that day when all of God's children, black men and white men, Jews and Gentiles, Protestants and

Catholics, will be able to join hands and sing in the words of the old Negro spiritual, "Free at last! Free at last! Thank God Almighty, we are free at last!"[3]

Some historians and political scientists consider this one of the most famous visionary speeches in history. No one can deny the power of King's vision. He deliberately exerted special influence to move the country in which he lived toward the goals that permanently fulfilled the country's real needs.

Lack of vision among leaders results in lethargy, confusion, disorder, inefficiency and—at worst—anarchy.

Leadership begins when a vision emerges. Proverbs 29:18 says, "Where there is no vision, the people perish" (KJV). The true meaning of these words is, "Without a vision, the people cast off restraint." Lack of vision among leaders results in lethargy, confusion, disorder, inefficiency and—at worst—anarchy. This applies in business as well as politics. A company unhitched from a clear vision is a company doomed to fail. Business leaders need to know where they are going, and they need the ability to communicate that direction in visionary decision making.

Visions Change the World

When John Sung returned to his native China in 1929, after having received his Ph.D. from Ohio State University, his preacher father said, "Good, John. Now, with your education, you can get an important teaching post and provide an education for your six brothers."

Most Chinese children obey the direct commands of their fathers. It's part of their Confucian heritage. It was unusual, therefore, for John to tell his father that he could not take a teaching post because God had called him to evangelize China and Southeast Asia. John had a vision of Chinese people becoming followers of Jesus Christ, and he believed he had only 15 years to fulfill that vision.

Over the next 15 years, John Sung did the work of a dozen men. And, in fact, he died at the end of those 15 years, in 1944. John Sung's vision drove him. That explains his feverish pace in carrying it out. Asia and the South Pacific are different today because of the ministry of John Sung. It all began with a vision translated into a mission and implemented by well-defined goals.

By their nature, visions look beyond today's situation:

- Mahatma Gandhi envisioned a free and independent India at a time when it was governed by the British.

- Henry Ford envisioned every family in America owning its own automobile at a time when most people were frightened of the new invention.

- William Wilberforce envisioned the abolition of slavery at a time when slaves were a profitable commodity in international trade.

- Daniel K. Ludwig envisioned a self-supporting industrial region in the heart of the Brazilian jungle at a time when there was no industry, no electricity, and no cities of any kind for hundreds of miles.

All these leaders had a clear picture of what their group would become or do as a result of the special influence they would exert. Even writers and artists often function as leaders in this respect. As visionary decisions go, few require greater commitment than the one that shuts you away to write a great novel or complete a great painting. And to see what kind of influence this achieves, you only have to go to your nearest bookshop or art gallery.

Wealthy and Corruption-free

The man who built Singapore, Lee Kuan Yew, must surely rank as one of the most important Asian leaders of the twentieth century.

Born in Singapore, he studied at the University of Cambridge in England, where he performed the almost impossible feat of passing first in the Law Tripos—above some of the best minds in the whole university.

Returning to Singapore, he founded the People's Action Party in 1954, entering the Singapore Legislative Assembly a year later. He became the country's first prime minister in 1959—a position he retained for the next 31 years. Believing that his country was not yet ready for independence, Lee decided to take Singapore into the Malaysian Federation in 1963. The experiment was short lived. Singapore was the only part of the federation with a Chinese majority, and racial tensions forced its withdrawal only two years later, "leaving Lee to govern an overcrowded, pestilential port with no major industry, no army, and no water supply."[4]

But Prime Minister Lee Kuan Yew had a vision for what Singapore could become. He envisaged a well-ordered society in which each individual could enjoy freedom to the maximum extent. In another person's hands, such a vision might never have been realized. Lee, however, turned his vision into a practical, long-term program of development.

Early on, for example, he sought the advice of the Dutch economist Albert Winsemius, who first came to Singapore in 1959 as leader of a United Nations Technical Assistance Board team. The story goes that Winsemius told Lee, "Whatever you do, make sure that you have a clean city and country. People from other parts of the world do not want to do business with a government whose municipalities are dirty." Since Lee had predicated his policy on the cornerstone of attracting foreign multinationals, he took the Dutchman's advice.

It worked.

Foreign investments and foreign multinationals drove Singapore's economic development in the 1970s and 1980s. Under Lee's wise and farsighted leadership, Singapore achieved its prime minister's multifaceted mission. It has a transparent and corruption-free civil service. Foreign investors have found that attractive. Singapore provides ample, decent, and affordable public housing. And it continues to expand its reputation as an international center for high-tech companies and financial services that demand high standards in health and education.

Today, despite its tiny size, Singapore has a per capita gross domestic product (GDP) equal to that of Europe's most developed nations. Inflation barely tops 2 percent. The last time I checked on Singapore Airlines, they had a $1.6 billion cash reserve, were enjoying a 24 percent return on their equity, and owned the newest fleet in the world. Singapore has overtaken Rotterdam as the world's largest and busiest port.

> *Worthy visions are a gift of God—*
> *even visions for business or politics.*

And this astounding change all began in the mind and heart of one ethnic Chinese, who delineated his vision and crafted the mission necessary to achieve it.

Visionary Decisions to Help You Define Your Vision

I believe that worthy visions are a gift of God—even visions for business or politics.

James said, "Every good gift and every perfect gift is from above, and comes down from the Father of lights, with whom there is no variation or shadow of turning" (James 1:17).

You don't have to believe in God to feel that way. Many people with visions, even atheists, will describe their vision as an "inspiration" or an "enlightenment." They sense that the vision has somehow come to them from elsewhere. They will also see the people they lead as a responsibility for which they are answerable.

We tend to compartmentalize our lives. We see God influencing only "spiritual" visions, missions, and goals, and keep our "secular" business under our own control. Yet St. Augustine said, "Let every Christian understand that wherever truth is found, it belongs to his Master." God is the God of *all* truth. And God is the source of *all* worthy visions.

In Korea, more than 500 years ago, King Sejong had a vision of an improved language for his people. King Sejong actualized his vision through a goals program that gave the Koreans the first alphabet in the Orient. He believed his vision came from God, and he successfully fulfilled it.

All business people understand the experience of having a sudden, great idea land on them as though out of nowhere. Sometimes a vision may lift you up and take you in a totally new direction. And sometimes you must look for it. So where to start?

Well, you start with a visionary decision to discover the details of what God has given you to do.

1. Define your vision by seeing what God has made you

The motivation specialist Paul J. Meyer started out without a dollar. At the age of 25 he had attained millionaire status. He had built the largest insurance agency in the world. He seemed to have nothing left to prove. But then a close friend challenged him: "Paul, you're happiest when you're helping others reach their full potential."

Paul J. Meyer caught the vision of motivating others and decided to leave the insurance business. In some ways, this was a risky move. Like all business start-ups, his new venture could have failed. Also, it seemed likely at first that he would never make as much money from it as he had made from insurance. Yet the vision gripped him. He knew what he must do.

Today, Paul Meyer's Success Motivation Institute has helped thousands. Leaders in more than 75 countries point to the SMI program as the instrument that opened a new world of possibility to them. The

SMI program has transformed some welfare recipients into corporate heads and university scholars.

*Very likely, the beginnings of a vision
lie within you long before you recognize it.*

Very often, those who feel called to a vision find, in that same calling, the strength to pull through when times are hard. If you don't believe in God, you will perhaps have a conviction that your vision is the right thing to do. It requires faith to cherish the vision and implement it.

Very likely, the beginnings of a vision lie within you long before you recognize it. Most people are so busy that their visions never register as more than a vague "If only..." or "Maybe one day it would be nice to..."

2. Define your vision by the immediate need

I recently toured facilities set up in South Africa by Haggai Institute alumnus Dr. Gustav du Toit.

By any criterion, Gustav qualifies as a world-class leader. What he showed me felt like a visit to hell and back. Many of those his organization cares for suffer from advanced AIDS, with no hope of a cure. The helpless victims include infant children, raped in the misguided belief that this act will cure an adult of HIV. Gustav himself has suffered assault, and his sister received a gunshot wound to the head.

Yet Gustav sticks resolutely to his God-appointed tasks: running a hospice, a school, and a church, and providing 48,000 hot meals per month to precious abused kids.

He told me that the hospice had served 344 patients in two years, and all had accepted Christ before dying. He is one of a number of wealthy, erudite, politically influential people in South Africa who have invested time, effort, prayer, and money for the nation's poor, ravaged, and hopeless.

Gustav du Toit would tell you he could not escape from his vision. The sheer scale of the need in South African society, with its extremes of wealth and poverty, bored into his soul and demanded a response.

3. Define your vision by solitude

You cannot focus on a vision when distractions interfere, any more than you can see the stars in the night sky when standing in New York's Times Square, Tokyo's Ginza, or London's Piccadilly Circus. You need solitude.

Cecil B. Day Sr., the creator and founder of Days Inn motels, liked to find his solitude in his shack at Tybee Beach near Savannah, Georgia. When the incoming tides at the Day Companies headquarters became crashing breakers, Cecil would go to Tybee. He would walk along the beach, letting the gentle waves cleanse his mind of the tension that clouded clear thinking. He loved the bustle of the headquarters building in Atlanta, but he couldn't do his best creative thinking in that atmosphere. After walking the deserted beaches, he returned to the city energetic and creative.

*I wrote as fast as I could, my thoughts
often tumbling ahead of my words.*

Day told me his vision for the motel chain came in solitude. At two o'clock one morning in 1970, he awakened, grabbed a notepad, and began writing. For 14 hours he penned the thoughts brimming over in his mind. When it was done, he had the core idea for the Days Inn motel. "The ideas were beyond my capacity," reported Cecil later. He clearly believed God had given him the vision. And it was a quality idea.

I had a similar experience in 1964. I made a visit to Beirut, which showed me some of the tensions created by neonationalism. I realized that Westerners wishing to contribute to the growth of the developing world would need to adopt a new approach.

Shortly after that visit, on the island of Bali in Indonesia, a fire began to burn in my soul. I told my three traveling companions that I would go "out of circulation" for a while. They understood and cooperated. I didn't leave my room. In absolute solitude, the vision that became Haggai Institute took shape in my mind. I wrote as fast as I could, my thoughts often tumbling ahead of my words. The informal creed I scribbled that day remains the one on which Haggai Institute functions.

Within the next twelve months, Jerry Beavan and my brother Tom Haggai made incisive and specific contributions to the outworking of the vision. But the core of it—the essential idea—came to me in complete solitude. Without that solitude, I would never have put together the thinking that finally made Haggai Institute work. Had I spent that holiday socializing, Haggai Institute would probably not exist.

Visions require a balance of action
and reflection, a blend of the
qualities of East and West.

Visions, then, require a balance of action and reflection, a blend of the qualities of East and West. Many years ago, an anthropologist told me, "The Western mind says, 'Don't just stand there—do something.' So, Westerners are action-oriented. The Eastern mind says, 'Don't do anything—just stand there.' So the Eastern mentality is more attuned to contemplation than action."

In a global economy, these qualities are beginning to mix. The East is becoming more action-oriented, and the West has started to see the value of contemplation. You must prepare for effective action by clear thinking. And you do your best thinking in solitude.

If you don't have the luxury of vacations where you can get away from others, find ways of creating your own solitude. Find time at the beginning of the day to do your undisturbed thinking. Or cultivate your inner solitude even in the midst of a noisy crowd.

Many times unforeseen events force a leader to make an immediate decision without the benefit of time to reflect and deliberate. At such moments, having the discipline of time spent regularly alone can pay big dividends. It ensures visionary decision making. It enables you to set a course and determine a plan of action without agonizing over each individual choice.

In Panama many years ago, a lady asked me, "Suppose at three o'clock this afternoon you face an unavoidable decision that would involve thousands of innocent lives and millions of dollars of other people's money. Suppose also that you had only two minutes to decide. What would you do?"

"I would follow my best judgment," I replied.

> *Jotting things down on a notepad serves far more than an aid to memory. It helps me tease out the details of the vision.*

She seemed surprised. She had expected me to say that I would try to compose myself mentally or pray.

"Dear lady," I said, "you have given me two minutes. It will consume every second of those two minutes to grasp as much of the relevant data as possible. I shall use my best judgment and trust that it proves correct.

"You see, this morning I had my quiet time with the Lord. I committed the day to Him. And He, Who knows the end from the beginning and with Whom there is no past, present, or future, has already prepared me. I therefore have full confidence that in this situation, my best judgment would reflect His will."

4. Define your vision by the discipline of writing

For me, jotting things down on a notepad serves far more than an aid to memory. It helps me tease out the details of the vision.

Peter and Mary Loring used the same method when they planned to set up a small retail business in Vermont, U.S.A. Their broker, Jim Howard, had himself discovered the benefits of writing, and now insisted on his clients using the same technique. The simple act of writing things down, he told the Lorings, would give them the guidelines on which to build their business.

The Lorings soon saw the wisdom of this advice.

"Once something comes down from your brain and through your hand onto a piece of paper," says Peter Loring, "you tend to remember it better. That helped us organize ourselves. You know, a lot of people get a whim to open a little store, but you need a lot more to make it happen."[5]

Writing imposed a discipline on them. It forced them to turn hazy ideas into concrete concepts. It showed them where they needed more information—for example, about their markets—and it provided them with material for a cogently written business plan. The plan duly impressed their banker.

Jim Howard insisted that all his clients go through the same painstaking process.

> He gave them questionnaires that forced them to write out responses to scores of ponderables. Why did they want to get into small business? What did they expect to bring to the experience? Writing down all the answers compelled them to think, and to be truthful with themselves, so that their plans would have a solid basis. The result? Howard's company wound up with prospective small business buyers who would not fail. By 1981, Howard was clinching a deal a week, and operating with an almost 100 percent success rate.[6]

According to Howard, writing is "the most intense form of self-examination I know. Most people try to get the same result from brainstorming, but talking is inherently deceptive, especially with the posturing that people do when they are part of a group. Writing serves as much more of an automatic filter. The single dimensional symbols involved screen out unimportant concepts. Put another way, they force you to be truthful."

> *The simple idea of writing out ideas*
> *is central to business success.*

Writing out my vision for Haggai Institute confirmed Howard's viewpoint. What finally came out of that dialogue with my notepad shaped a crisp and an exacting document. True, I made some changes later on. I also took on fresh perspectives from trusted friends and critics. But the nub of the idea got hammered out by writing alone.

Howard sees the simple idea of writing out ideas as central to business success.

"If you look at some notable failures in American business in the last three decades, what you can trace to all of them—the design mania in autos in the 1950s that produced so many useless cars, the more quiet decline of quality in manufactured goods—is the result of a lack of hard introspection. When you write things out, you really see what's important and what isn't. And when you know what is important, you have real power."

Successful use of writing, according to Howard, comes down to eight main points:

- Profitable writing requires complete solitude and regular practice.
- Be prepared to go through 100 pages of nonsense to find one page of value in what you've written.
- You have to eliminate your pride of ownership over what you've written or you'll never be properly objective about it.
- Have a sense of humor about what you've written.

- Approach a piece of writing with some understandable focus for it while never forfeiting your spontaneity within the process.

- Your goal in writing out your thoughts and feelings must matter enough to justify the pain and honesty involved.

- Pay attention to the format and the words you use; they're clues to what you are actually doing.

- Keep writing until you get the vision clear.

5. Define your vision by tough questions

Sometimes it helps to have someone help you drive your thinking.

Peter Daniels of Adelaide, Australia, helps people realize their potential in this way. He has demonstrated by his own experience how much hidden potential a person can possess. At 26, he could neither read nor write. He was profane, broke, and belligerent. He had been tossed from one broken home to another. Then, suddenly, he had a spiritual experience that made him change his ways.

Peter Daniels became wealthy, literate, influential, and one of Australia's outstanding speakers and international board members. And he has analyzed the problems of those who, like him, have yearned for meaning in their lives. He recommends they ask four key questions:[7]

- What is the age you have set as your goal for reaching your full potential?

- What is your full potential in every area of your life? Write that down, in 50 pages or more. (Daniels requires at least 50 pages. Otherwise, a person could put down a few words, which, he says, would be "frivolous." Forcing people to write at least 50 pages measures the sincerity of their concern.)

- If your full potential is 100 percent, what percentage rating do you give yourself right now?

- Given the difference between your current rating and the 100 percent, what plan have you made to bridge the gap, and when will you accomplish that plan?

Responding to these four questions could take the better part of a day. But when a person responds fully and honestly, a clear picture of his situation emerges. Peter Daniels' four questions are designed to develop what I call *inspirational dissatisfaction*. They show clearly what you could achieve if you lived at your full potential. And they show what you are now. Without inspirational dissatisfaction, a person will make peace with the status quo. He will not see a need for change, and will not feel a motive for realizing a vision.

Inspirational dissatisfaction can develop a positive mood. It impels you forward and makes you determined. It does not engender a morose, brooding, cynical restlessness that inclines you to withdraw and hide. Nor is it an aggressive resentment that blames other people for your problems but does nothing to improve your lot. Inspirational dissatisfaction inspires a person to high attainment.

6. Define your vision by God's mandate

If God takes you seriously enough to entrust you with a vision, then you must take yourself seriously.

You cannot separate leadership from vision. Realizing a vision means realizing your potential to pursue that vision and see it bear fruit. If a leader has a vision but does not take his potential seriously, that vision will soon die. It will remain a dream.

Like Isaiah, you may want to say, "Woe is me, for I am undone! Because I am a man of unclean lips. And I dwell in the midst of a people of unclean lips" (Isaiah 6:5). You may feel, like Moses at the burning bush, unqualified for the assignment.

God never assigns a task and then deprives
His agent of the tools required to complete it.

But God will work through you, in spite of all your inadequacies, if you have faith in His power. God never assigns a task and then deprives His agent of the tools required to complete it.

Visions don't require experience. They don't require academic degrees. The key word is *potential*. Your vision may take you into an area you have never been in before. You will need to learn new skills. What matters, then, is not what you know already, but how much confidence and self-belief you have based on your faith in God. Those will help you make the vision real.

In a vision given by God, the apostle Peter learned that the Gospel was for the Gentiles as well as for the Jews. Under the leadership of the Holy Spirit, he then had to sell that vision to his colleagues.

Dwight L. Moody had a vision of building a Bible institute that would train laypeople to become effective in evangelism. It was a new concept. God gave Moody, the businessman turned evangelist, the vision. Then Moody had to light the flame so that others could see the vision and commit to the mission.

God gave Dr. Han Kyung Chik a vision of a church in Seoul, Korea, at the end of World War II. Initially, only 27 people—all refugees—shared his vision. Years later, the church stood 60,000 strong, built not by one person but by many followers who caught the vision of Dr. Han.

A vision generates direction, order, devotion. It overcomes aimlessness, chaos, lawlessness. But a leader must also feel an inspirational dissatisfaction, a determination to change things, and a certainty that he himself can function as the agent of change—even if he does not yet have the necessary resources or skills.

When You Reach the "Commit" Moment

By the time you have sacrificed significant time to capture a vision you will already feel a strong commitment to it. The vision resembles a newborn baby. Just holding it brings tremendous satisfaction. But it also brings a huge responsibility. This is the point to commit—one hundred percent.

A vision resembles a newborn baby.
Just holding it brings tremendous satisfaction.
But it also brings a huge responsibility.

In 1929, Will H. Houghton, pastor of the 4000-member Baptist Tabernacle in Atlanta, Georgia, was visiting Europe with his wife and her mother. Halfway through the scheduled itinerary, Houghton felt a compulsion to return to America at once.

He didn't know why, but he knew God was directing him to return. He left his wife and mother-in-law to finish the trip, while he took a fast ship to New York. He arrived on a Wednesday in time to attend the midweek prayer service at Calvary Baptist Church across the street from Carnegie Hall. The pastor, John Roach Straton, had just become seriously ill, and Houghton was asked if he would fill the pulpit temporarily. He returned to Calvary Baptist Church in January 1930, preaching in the city often dubbed "the graveyard of preachers." Straton died in October 1930, and Houghton accepted the invitation to the pastorate. He was one of the few who thrived as a preacher in New York City.

From Calvary's highly visible pulpit, Houghton came to the attention of James M. Gray, the 84-year-old president of Moody Bible Institute. Gray became convinced that Houghton should follow him as president and reported his conviction to the board of trustees. Houghton served as president of Moody Bible Institute until 1946. Had Houghton ignored the vision, he probably would never have fulfilled his leadership potential. However, because of his sensitivity, he was put in a position of leadership where he had a world-changing impact on the lives of millions for the glory of God.

If God has put a vision in your heart, accept the presence of this desire as His oath that it can find fulfillment—and commit yourself to the task.

Vision begets action. God gave Noah the vision of an ark, and he built it. God gave Nehemiah a vision of a city wall, and he repaired it. God gave Paul the apostle a vision of evangelizing the whole world, and he covered the earth with the message of Christ. God gave David Livingstone a vision of Africa, and he opened the way for thousands of missionaries to preach the Gospel.

If God has put a vision in your heart, accept the presence of this desire as His oath that it can find fulfillment—and commit yourself to the task. Failure to act on your vision can lead to personal stagnation, a troubled spirit, and a critical attitude. A God-given vision is an awesome responsibility. Fulfillment can lead you to the heights of tremendous service to God and to people. Failure to follow the vision will deprive others of the leadership they need.

No Vision Comes Free

Of course the "commit" moment has a flipside: you must be ready to pay the price. I'll be frank. Following your vision can cost you. Just take a glance at the pages of history.

In 1774 and 1775, the American colonies prepared to break away from England. Confusion, disagreement, and rancor threatened to undermine the Continental Convention. Yet many of the participants had a clear vision and credited it to God.

Benjamin Franklin told the Convention, "I believe that Providence guides the affairs of men, and never a sparrow falls to the ground that God does not attend its funeral, and that all the hairs of our heads are numbered. I don't believe that an empire or a republic can be launched without His help, and I move, Mr. President, that this convention open with prayer and that we petition Divine guidance and help in the step we are about to take."

Visions have consequences. To pursue and achieve a vision you may have to suffer for it.

Visions have consequences. To pursue and achieve a vision you may have to suffer for it. The signatories of the Declaration of Independence knew this only too well. They were subjects of the King of England. Therefore the act of signing the Declaration turned them instantly into traitors. Nearly all of them were to pay for their courage.

Francis Lewis, a New York delegate, saw his home plundered and his estate, in what is now Harlem, completely destroyed by British soldiers. William Floyd, another New York delegate, was able to escape with his wife and children across Long Island Sound to Connecticut, where they lived as refugees without income for seven years. Dr. John Witherspoon, president of the College of New Jersey, later called Princeton, saw the country's finest college library burned. Judge Richard Stockton was pulled from his bed in the night and brutally beaten by the arresting soldiers. Thrown into a common jail, he was deliberately starved.

You may think I'm going a little over the top in emphasizing the cost of leadership. Most visions will not set a team of assassins on your tail. But don't accept a vision casually. Tough challenges will lie ahead. Without wholehearted and realistic commitment to a vision, you will never see it through, and you will never practice real leadership. You may occupy a leadership position. But you will not be an influential leader.

Don't confuse leadership with management.

Don't confuse leadership with management. Though a manager can keep an operation running, only an influential leader can motivate people to accomplish those changes that meet their real needs. I'm not putting managers down; the world needs good managers. Management, though, is not leadership.

Do all influential leaders stand at the top of large corporations? Not at all. The "smaller" visions are no less important. A father or mother may have a vision for the education of their children, and this will have a huge influence because parents can play such a powerful role in the formation of their children's attitudes and personalities. A wise parent moves the family toward the fulfillment of a vision—and the fulfillment of their real needs.

After the Vision...What?

The Olympic Games 2008 may mark the point at which the rest of the world woke up to the emergence of China as a world power.

I am a veteran student of China. Over the last two decades, I have visited the country at least twice a year. And I have stood in awe at the strides being made by this ancient nation. You only have to drive across the bridge linking Shanghai and Pudong to see how skillfully the economic growth and infrastructure have been kept in equilibrium.

These changes did not happen by chance. They date back to 1979, originating in the vision of China's paramount leader, Deng Xiaoping. That vision could have remained a dream. In fact, though, the Chinese leadership translated it into a nuts-and-bolts mission that included increased productivity in agriculture, the building of great cities, and the establishment of a viable market economy.

Visions find expression in visionary decisions. And the next decision you make must amount to an overarching plan of implementation—a set of final, practical objectives that embody the vision. In common parlance, a mission.

Nehemiah had a vision of a rebuilt wall around Jerusalem. At the time, Nehemiah worked 930 miles (1500 kilometers) from his homeland. The holy city of Jerusalem had been captured decades before, and much of it destroyed. Nehemiah himself was a servant and cup-bearer to King Artaxerxes of Persia. And yet, from these apparently unpromising beginnings, Nehemiah forged a mission to rebuild the walls of Jerusalem for the glory of God. Read the book of Nehemiah to see one of the oldest records of visionary decision making.

Leap forward two and half millennia to the American space program of the 1960s. At the beginning of that decade, President John Kennedy challenged the American people with a dream of putting an American on the moon in ten years. That was a vision. Almost immediately, the government launched a program designed to accomplish that vision—the Apollo mission.

At age ten, God blessed me by giving me my life's vision—the evangelization of the world.

In both these cases, only laying out a series of specific, measurable intermediary steps could fulfill the vision and achieve the mission.

Out of the mission you determine the goals needed to carry out the mission. This exercise, requiring unrelenting discipline, ignites visionary decision making.

At age ten, God blessed me by giving me my life's vision—the evangelization of the world. I visualized people enslaved by sin, darkness, and fear now liberated. I saw them enjoying a life of faith and fulfillment under the lordship of Jesus Christ. I committed myself to the implementation of that vision. That vision took specific shape in the idea of providing leadership training for effective evangelism—my mission.

A mission without supporting goals matures into sheer fantasy that eventuates in frustration. So I proceeded to lay down concrete goals. The goals clustered together in numerous groups. For example:

- Finding and maintaining buildings in Singapore and Maui to house Haggai Institute (material goals)

- Reading three books a week to keep myself up-to-date (mental goals)
- Building friendships with people who could share my vision and mission (social goals)
- Raising funds to support the work of the Institute (financial goals)

The influential leader meticulously details action steps for each goal.

Goals achieve nothing unless you develop action steps. As Eric Haas says, "A goal without a plan is a wish without a hope." You must break down these action steps into time-sensitive, prioritized steps.

Each of the above goals found support in detailed plans involving place, time, relationships, individuals and foundations to contact, and prayer support—both individual and corporate.

Influential leaders grasp and cherish a vision.
They think on it by day and dream of it by night.

My vision has dominated my life. That's what visions should do. Influential leaders grasp and cherish a vision. They implement it through visionary decision making. They think on it by day and dream of it by night.

Continuously thinking about the vision induces action. It sounds the death knell to complacency. As the psalmist said, "My heart was hot within me; while I was musing, the fire burned" (Psalm 39:3).

Summary

Leadership begins with a vision. A vision provides a clear picture of what the leader sees his group being or doing. A vision could focus on health where sickness afflicts, on knowledge where ignorance prevails, on freedom where oppression reigns, or on love where hatred dominates. The leader commits wholeheartedly to his vision, which involves beneficial change for his group.

Influential leaders understand the importance of vision and make it the driving force behind leadership. Yet the vision will achieve nothing if a leader does not take the next step of concretizing objectives that will lead to the vision's realization.

Visions do not simply spring from the unconscious mind. They are given—whether the leader thinks in spiritual terms or not. The influential leader takes his vision seriously. But he also takes himself seriously. Not out of excessive self-regard or personal vanity, but because every vision makes demands of the visionary.

The vision will remain a dream unless you, the leader, have the passion and determination to make that vision real. Feeling unprepared does not matter. Far more important is to find and grasp the potential within you to see the vision realized.

In seizing a vision, solitude offers enormous benefits. If you are constantly in the company of others, you will not see the vision. You will be too busy, and other people's thoughts and ideas will dominate your mind. So make sure you spend time in solitude. Make a few minutes every day where you can sit alone with your thoughts. And use writing to clarify and purify your thinking. With this method, you will achieve the inspiration you are looking for.

STEP 2

DECIDE TO ACHIEVE
WHAT YOU AIM FOR

In 1950, Yale University began a longitudinal study of its students. In the initial survey, only 3 percent of those graduating reported writing out career goals. At completion 25 years later, the study revealed an extraordinary fact: the 3 percent who'd written out their goals now owned *97 percent of the wealth earned by all surviving members of the group.*

Discovering a vision is important. But it won't change anything if you stay stuck on the starting blocks. You need to translate the vision into concrete objectives—a mission you can pursue by means of a sequence of specific goals.

Cecil Day (referred to in the previous chapter) had a vision of developing a chain of low-cost hotels. In concrete terms that translated into a business plan for the Days Inns motel business. In four years, he built 40,000 rooms. As far as I know, that achievement has never been equaled.

Less than five years later, an international oil embargo caused a scarcity of gasoline that lowered highway traffic volume dramatically. This cut into Days Inns' revenue. Furthermore, the hike in oil prices froze liquidity across the country. When the motels under construction at the time of the oil crisis were completed, the banks had no money to fulfill their commitment for conventional loans. As a result, Cecil was saddled with high-interest construction loans.

Through all this, he never lost his vision. But he re-engineered his mission and goals. He visited three bankers a day, five days a week for 21 months. He kept adjusting his goals with new, well-thought-out action steps that would make his vision a reality. When he died in 1978, the entire business flourished, and his vision had been carried out.

The influential leader will embrace the vision. But that vision must find expression in the language of mission. It's the difference between an architect's sketch and the final blueprint. And that blueprint boils down to a series of specific, measurable steps by which you can turn your empty lot into a finished building. A leader without goals resembles a ship's captain without a compass or a truck driver without a map or signposts.

Effective implementation of the vision depends heavily on the skill of goal setting.

Effective implementation of the vision, then, depends heavily on the skill of goal setting. The clearer the leader's goals, the sharper his focus and the more likely he is to realize his vision. Effective goal setting focuses the leader's vision by spelling out what steps he will take to accomplish it.

The industrialist Henry J. Kaiser said, "Determine what you want more than anything else in life, write down the means by which you intend to attain it, and permit nothing to deter you from pursuing it."

That means an influential leader will do goal setting as if it were second nature. For this reason, I want to look at it carefully. It's vital to understand why goal setting matters and how to set goals that will help you achieve what you aim for.

What's the Point of a Plan?

Keep in your mind the three reasons to do goal setting.

First, goal setting helps you succeed—as shown dramatically by the Yale University study cited at the start of this chapter.

Second, goals govern your whole approach to achievement. Leaders may dither over hard decisions. A clear vision and goal structure cuts through the dithering. Does a certain move assist in the accomplishing of a goal? Then do it. Does it take the organization off in a different and irrelevant direction? Then let the opportunity go by. In this way, the leader conserves energy by concentrating on well-defined goals.

Most stress comes from confusion and fear. Goals tend to eliminate confusion and override fear.

Third, goal setting contributes to a healthier lifestyle. Most stress comes from confusion and fear. Goals tend to eliminate confusion and override fear. The performance psychiatrist who advises the world's leading stock traders, Ari Kiev, says:

> I have repeatedly found that helping people to develop personal goals has proved to be the most effective way to help them to cope with problems and maximize their satisfaction... With goals, people can overcome confusion and conflict over incompatible values, contradictory desires, and frustrated relationships...all of which often result from the absence of rational life strategies. Without a central goal [a mission], your thoughts may become worrisome; your confidence and morale may be undermined, and you may be led to the feared circumstances. Without a goal, you will focus on your weaknesses, and the possibilities of errors and criticism. This will foster indecision, procrastination, and inadequacy and will impede the development of your potential.[8]

John Wesley, though assaulted, beaten, and maligned, remained calm and cheerful. Goals kept him stress-free. He could say, with Paul the apostle, "I consider that the sufferings of this present time are not worthy to be compared with the glory which shall be revealed in us" (Romans 8:18).

Some of the world's leading medical experts emphasize the importance of goals as a deterrent to sickness and as a stabilizer of health. The authors of *Getting Well Again,* a groundbreaking book, argue that goal setting and striving constitute one of the most important and successful therapies in combating cancer. They say that setting new life goals constitutes the most effective tool for getting patients well. As they conceptualize and visualize their reasons for living, patients reinvest themselves in life.[9]

Goals also help to provide a sense of accomplishment. Psychological satisfaction depends on feeling that your life is worthwhile. In turn, that feeling is reinforced strongly if you can point to goals you have recently attained. Even if you have not yet completed your mission, you know that certain key stages have already been reached.

Visionary Decisions to Help You Achieve What You Aim For

Paul J. Meyer, founder of the internationally renowned Success Motivation Institute, says emphatically: "If you are not what you ought to be, want to be, or could be, it's because you have not clearly defined your goals."

Many writers and instructors now promote goal setting, so much so that we think we are setting goals when really we are not. So what makes for effective goal setting?

Here is a set of goals I wrote out for running a leadership training seminar:

- Determine the objective of the seminar in precise detail.

- Determine the faculty.
- Determine the participants.
- Determine the length of the sessions and the length of the entire seminar.
- Determine the funding required.
- Enlist the faculty.
- Secure the facilities.
- Secure the appropriate materials and equipment.
- Produce the necessary funding.
- Select the candidates requesting the advanced training.

First, take note that these goals interrelate. Some depend on others, and nearly all of them depend on funding.

Second, note that you must break down each goal into a series of subgoals with specific and detailed plans. You must not take anything for granted or omit any detail. Thomas Carlyle said, "Genius is the infinite capacity for taking pains."

You must analyze your goals carefully and subject them to constant review.

Don't confuse a goals program, a program of work, with a wish list. You must analyze your goals carefully and subject them to constant review. The influential leader accepts this and knows how to make it work—because his vision depends on it. His goal program turns into a to-do list, to examine and check daily. Daily review ensures that something gets imbedded not only in your conscious but also in your subconscious mind.

Resolve to make ten visionary decisions to help you achieve what you aim for.

1. Achieve what you aim for by making goals specific

You don't construct a legitimate goal by writing "I want to make my department more efficient." That may reflect a valid desire, but it doesn't point you to any precise action. Rather, state your goal as: "I want to achieve greater efficiency by cutting my costs." Expressed like this, the goal defines the action you need to take.

Make your goals tangible. If you find your impatience a negative, and you determine to change your behavior, you must convert the intangible desire to tangible steps. You could set yourself a goal of "being more patient." But how do you know whether or not you have succeeded? Can you visualize this goal? Can you measure it? Can you monitor it? How do you move toward achieving it?

If you want to develop greater patience, act on this intangible goal by using tangible action steps. For instance:

- I won't complain for the next ten days when my wife is late.

- I won't honk my horn today when another driver annoys me.

- On this journey, I will smile if my plane is delayed and I may miss an important engagement.

- When an employee repeats a mistake this week, I will quietly and kindly repeat the correct instructions.

- I will devote the first 30 minutes of each day to a quiet time of Bible reading and prayer.

- I will not only give the first part of each day to spiritual matters, but I will also devote the first day of each week and the first tenth of every dollar to the Lord and His work.

- I will tell someone what the Lord has done for me at least five days out of every week.

- At least once a week I'll inconvenience myself, if need be, to visit someone in need, for the purpose of encouraging and helping that person in Jesus' name.

2. Achieve what you aim for by making your goals measurable

Tangible goals are easy to assess because you can measure your performance. "If you can't measure it, you can't monitor it," says Paul J. Meyer. He's right.

> *Only when you can measure a goal*
> *will you know when you've achieved it.*

So, put figures to your goal. You want to cut your budget. By exactly how much? Five hundred dollars a month? One hundred? Only when you can measure the goal will you know when you've achieved it.

Take the phrase "significant savings." How do you define "significant savings"? Can you quantify "significant savings"? What does it boil down to in hard currency? If you have numbers, you will know whether you have succeeded. If you don't succeed, you will know by exactly how much you missed the target.

You measure goals in two ways. First, by specifying *what* you will accomplish. Second, by specifying *when* you will accomplish it.

Are you aiming to save $5000 over a year or a month or a week? Clearly, the time scale makes a huge difference. Also, the time it takes you to complete this goal will affect the next goal down the line. Often, work on a second goal cannot start until the first goal has been accomplished.

3. Achieve what you aim for by making your goals unrealistic

When I first talked about goal setting I laid great emphasis on making the goals realistic. Only a couple of years ago, after a lifetime of setting goals, did it occur to me that I'd never set a realistic goal in my life. My life's motto violates the idea of a realistic goal: "Attempt something so great for God, it is doomed to failure unless God be in it."

As a young man, John D. Rockefeller often annoyed his friends by saying, "One day, I am going to have a hundred thousand dollars!" At that time, he and his friends were all junior shipping clerks, with barely enough income to pay for their lodgings. Rockefeller had set an unrealistic goal. Within ten years he had made, not a hundred thousand dollars but several million!

> *Embrace a goal that stretches you beyond*
> *the limit. Then chart your course to get there.*

True, the world is full of gamblers with exactly the same goal Rockefeller had. But they don't set goals. "Unrealistic goal setting" breaks the bonds of the realistic. I'm not talking about a wish. Embrace a goal that stretches you beyond the limit. Then chart your course to get there. The higher you aim, the further you will go—every time.

4. Achieve what you aim for by making your goals attainable

Look carefully at your resources for filling the gap of current reality and your goal. What do you have the time to do? What do you have the money to do? What do you have the friends and contacts to do? How can you leverage these resources in a way that propels you toward your goal?

Let me explain what I mean by attainable. In writing this book, I set myself the target of one chapter per month. I could have aimed for two chapters, but given the rest of my schedule, that would have put the goal beyond my reach. I know I can write a chapter a month if I am sufficiently disciplined. Consequently, the way I structured my goals sharpened my focus and intensified my concentration.

Christians can find this subject difficult. We are to have faith in God. And we are told that with His power all things are possible. To what extent should we presume on God's assistance?

Moses sent 12 spies from Kadesh Barnea to spy out the land. They reported a land flowing with milk and honey and abounding in incomparable fruit. They all agreed it was a desirable land, but ten of the spies soured the report and terrified the Israelites by their description of the giants in the land (Numbers 13:31-33). "We are not able to go up against the people," they said.

However, two of the spies, Caleb and Joshua, brought the minority report. They, too, saw the giants, but they insisted the land was God's provision and He would see them through to victory. The goals of Joshua and Caleb were unattainable by human ability. But moving forward by faith in God, they proved the seemingly unattainable decidedly attainable.

Forty years later, the Lord permitted only Caleb and Joshua to enter the Promised Land. The other ten spies never made it.

5. Achieve what you aim for by limiting your goals to things you can control

I can list a score of hospitals, universities, and charitable organizations that based their goals on hoped-for money from wealthy people—money that never materialized.

> *Ideally, you base your goals on factors under your control.*

Many leaders have been seriously detained in the pursuit of worthwhile goals because they overestimated their employees' work rate or capability. In some instances, the leaders themselves failed. They failed to provide sufficient training or proper supervision. They did not insist on periodic performance reviews.

Ideally, you base your goals on factors under your control. In most businesses, a manager can direct people's work even if he cannot motivate them. In nonprofits, volunteer workers often fail to measure up to the employed personnel. So don't make unrealistic assumptions about other people's skills or motivation.

6. Achieve what you aim for by detailing your goals in writing

Lord Bacon said, "Writing makes an exact man." He was right. Writing crystallizes your thoughts and makes your ideas specific. Writing also aids your memory. It also has the power of bringing thoughts into a visual pattern and making important connections. Often I find that new ideas emerge when I express my goals in writing.

A leader becomes more effective when he or she assists memory by keeping a written record. When you write, you engage the power of your senses. You use the sense of vision by seeing what you're writing. You use the sense of touch, feeling the pen or keyboard. You use the sense of smell, taking in the subliminal odors of ink or electrical circuitry. You use the sense of hearing—the sound of the writing instrument on the paper or the clicking of the keys. In all these ways you engage physically as well as mentally with the system of goals you are laying out.

Starting a good habit works far better than trying to shake a bad one.

Remember that a goals program may cover five, ten, or twenty years, and that even the most agile mind may lose touch with detail if that detail isn't accurately recorded. Construct a written action plan for every goal. Consider the mission as a ladder and the goals as the rungs. Make sure you have properly spaced the rungs and made them sufficiently strong—otherwise the ladder will not help you.

7. Achieve what you aim for by stating your goals positively

Starting a good habit works far better than trying to shake a bad one. To set a goal like "I will stop procrastinating" will usually have little effect. It focuses on the negative. You direct your attention to the thing you want to stop.

Say, instead, "I will be decisive." This readies your mind for a positive move. It challenges your creativity. It delivers a sense of immediate accomplishment when you reach the goal by making a quick and effective decision.

Evangelist D.L. Moody asked a pathetically small audience, "How many of you believe God can fill the 5000 chairs in this hall?" Every hand went up.

"How many of you believe God *will* fill the chairs in this hall with people?" Fewer than 30 hands went up.

"You see," he chided, "it takes no faith to say God *can* do it; it takes great faith to say God *will* do it."

> *Make your goals the expression of your noblest qualities—a desire to achieve your maximum for God.*

Let your mind soar. Make your goals the expression of your noblest qualities—a desire to live and achieve your maximum for God.

8. Achieve what you aim for by focusing on behavioral changes

You'll find some goals impossible to reach without first addressing flaws in your behavior.

For example, you can't expect to lose weight (if that is your goal) when you have an uncontrollable craving for fatty foods. You must change your behavior first. Similarly, you can't launch a new program or enterprise if you permit fear of risk to paralyze you. You must begin by targeting a behavioral change that controls your risk-aversion level.

Usually, people in business tackle goals they set themselves more effectively than they tackle goals set by others. This principle holds true at all levels in an organization. As far as possible, then, ensure that every person in the organization sets his or her own goals in the context of the goals of the enterprise.

The leader can provide guidance for goal setting. But if staff members set their own goals, the leader can have greater confidence that he will achieve his overall targets. Also, by promoting personal accountability in this way, he reduces the risk of staff members blaming each other if they fall short.

9. Achieve what you aim for by watching out for goal conflicts

Writing down your goals allows you to establish priorities when two desirable goals come into conflict.

A common form of conflict involves inadvertently double-counting resources such as time and money. Paying for a new home may conflict with paying to send your children to university. In such cases, your value system will determine which option you see as more important.

Conflicts of goals can also occur because two people are pursuing the same vision in different ways. As a business leader your goals will include achieving maximum output for minimum cost. Your employees, however, may see things differently. They may value job security, prospects for advancement, or a good salary. This does not mean they disagree with the overall corporate vision. But it may affect their priorities and their willingness to make sacrifices for the sake of the company. Only good leadership can resolve the conflict and move the organization forward.

Harold Geneen, former chief executive officer of corporate giant ITT, says:

Leadership is the ability to inspire other people to work together as a team under your direction, in order to attain a common objective, whether in business, in politics, in war, or on the football field. No one can possibly do it all alone. Others in the organization must want to follow your lead.[10]

The leader challenges people to work at those goals that fulfill a vision. Geneen says, "I wanted to get people to reach for goals that they might have thought were beyond them. I wanted them to accomplish more than they thought possible. And I wanted them to do it not only for the company and their careers, but for the fun of it."

You need to review your goals frequently in order to adjust them to changing situations.

Another form of goal conflict can occur in your own mind. Alongside your formal goal plan you may have other off-budget goals that nevertheless make demands on your time and resources. A lot of people overestimate the time they can spend with their families when heavy work schedules preempt free time. Failure to address this goal conflict puts you in the realm of wishful thinking, false promises, imposing disappointment on those close to you, and putting even greater strain on key relationships.

10. Achieve what you aim for by keeping your goals flexible

Note that goals need far greater flexibility than visions and missions. The vision remains the same, and the mission corresponds to the vision. But you need to review the goals frequently in order to adjust them to changing situations.

For example, assume you have a vision to develop the finest secondary school in the city. You realistically expect that it will take eight years to accomplish this mission. For each year, you will need to establish a series of goals for the faculty, student body, curriculum, physical facilities, public relations, and other areas.

The first year you may target three teachers with master's degrees, a student-teacher ratio of 30:1 or lower, and 20 percent of the faculty participating in continuing education. By the fourth year, however, those goals will have changed. You will probably aim to have ten teachers with masters' degrees, a student-teacher ratio of 22:1 or lower, and 35 percent of the faculty participating in continuing education.

In America in the early 1900s, business gurus considered the Pennsylvania Railroad the most successful business in the nation. Financial advisors often counseled a widow to invest her money in Pennsylvania Railroad stock. They assured her, "You can always count on the Old Pennsy."

But the railroad business was moving into obsolescence almost as fast as the horse and cart. Railroad businesses like the Old Pennsy collapsed because executives could not adjust their goals to serve the long-term vision.

If you had asked the executives of the Pennsylvania Railroad, "What is your business?" they would have answered, "Railroads." They should have said "Transportation." They then could have expanded their business to include heavy trucking, highways, jumbo jets, buses, and helicopters. But these railroad men remained, as Harvard professor Theodore Levitt has written, "imperturbably self-confident." They also lost the business.

Keep the vision permanent and goals flexible.

In business, as in any other enterprise, keep the vision permanent and goals flexible. But often it turns out the other way around. The goals become fixed and vision lapses. Businesses cling to old buildings, old markets, old structures—long after these have fallen into terminal decline. They ignore the constantly changing market. In business, you must keep your goals in sync with constant changes or face financial decline, even bankruptcy.

While you are working on your immediate goals, make sure to keep your eyes on your long-range goals too.

I cannot insist too strongly that setting goals constitutes an ongoing discipline. You must constantly modify your goals to keep them in sync with the ever-changing conditions. Stay on top of your goals so that the changing environment won't catch you by surprise. And while you are working on your immediate goals, make sure to keep your eyes on your long-range goals too.

How to Get Started

Here's the way I did it.

Once I had clearly understood my vision and framed it in concrete terms as a mission, I set myself the task of working out the details. Every day I would take a lined paper pad and write down every conceivable step toward the accomplishment of the mission. I cannot refer you to any particular logic or sequence. I wrote as fast as the ideas came to my head.

Prior to each of these sessions, which lasted anywhere from 15 minutes to an hour and a half, I had my quiet time and earnestly asked God to guide me. I took great comfort in the words of James: "If any of you lacks wisdom, let him ask of God, who gives to all liberally and without reproach, and it will be given to him" (James 1:5). And I kept reminding the Lord that I qualified for that wisdom because I lacked it.

Every week or so I would review the items I had written down. I would eliminate some, combine some, and alter some. In reviewing,

I would come up with other ideas. This continued for the better part of a year.

In addition to the items I had written down, I made a list of my assets and a list of liabilities. I wrote down every quality or performance I could think of that indicated a personal liability, as well as every criticism I could remember. On the other side of the sheet, I wrote down every asset as I perceived it. In addition, I listed every commendation I had received. This helped me understand myself as never before, and it helped me delineate the life mission to which I felt God had called me.

I blush with embarrassment when I confess that not until my 30s did I sort out the goals by which I would accomplish my life mission. I specified the achievements I felt necessary—both personal achievements and achievements of others working with me.

If goal setting accomplishes so much,
why don't more people set goals?

I covered every conceivable area of life, including place of residence, personal lifestyle, travel requirements, mental development, social activities, financial goals, family goals, organizational goals, and spiritual goals. Some items I found mutually exclusive. Then I had to determine my value system and make a decision about priorities.

Do You Have Goal Phobia?

If goal setting accomplishes so much, why don't more people set goals?

Some opine that effective goal setting takes effort. It takes determination. It takes commitment. And it also takes an ability to sidestep your fears.

Ponder four particular anxieties that keep some people back from the discipline of a goals program.

Fear of setting bad goals

Some avoid setting goals in case those goals prove fragmentary or inaccurate. Actually, perfection in goal setting can never be attained, almost by definition. Life changes, contexts change—and you must adapt your goals accordingly. Also, don't feel thwarted if you never get 100 percent of the way to a given goal. At worst, you will find yourself a lot further ahead than you would have been without setting goals.

Fear of failing

At some time or another, everyone sets a goal he fails to reach. Does that reality give grounds to abandon setting goals? Everyone who rides a bicycle has fallen off it. Is that a reason to abandon cycling as a form of transportation or recreation?

---

*An ordinary person fails and gives up;
the true leader examines the causes
and resumes his quest.*

Accidents happen. Everyone makes mistakes. But where an ordinary person fails and gives up, the true leader examines the causes and resumes his quest. In that context of constructive persistence, defeat converts into character building.

Defeat becomes a destructive force only when a person interprets it as failure. When you interpret defeat as a needed lesson, it rises to the level of a blessing. From my study of history, I have concluded those who face the most obstacles go on to score the most achievements.

Fear of ridicule

At age 22, I bought a book called *Thirty Days to a More Powerful Vocabulary.*[11] I realized that the larger a person's vocabulary, the wider the scope and the deeper the penetration of his thinking. One cannot think beyond the limit of the words used to grasp and express thought.

Unfortunately, I employed the new and fancy words I was learning a bit too freely. As a result, some people chided me. One said, "To understand John Haggai, you need to carry a *Webster's Unabridged Dictionary.*" That hurt!

Just as I was about to abandon my vocabulary-building discipline, a friend said to me, "John, I notice you're working on your vocabulary." I winced. But he went on, "Don't be embarrassed. I admire you. At first you may use new words awkwardly. But I want to encourage you not only to proceed, but also to maintain the discipline as long as you live. It will widen your capacity for knowledge and understanding."

The moment you set a goal,
you will confront opposition.

Prior to that encounter, I had abandoned the idea of pursuing speed-reading and memory courses. But after overcoming the fear of ridicule, I proceeded with both.

The moment you set a goal, you will confront opposition. Why? Often because of jealousy. "Other people know they should be doing the same thing," a friend said to me. "It annoys them that you're a step ahead. Recognize ridicule, then, as a disguised compliment."

Fear of presumption

Some may not set goals because of the verse that says, "Keep back Your servant also from presumptuous sins" (Psalm 19:13). But goal setting meshes perfectly with the sovereignty of God.

Several years ago I was lecturing to a group of Brazilian Christian leaders. We had been discussing goals as they related to the number of people we wanted to see evangelized in the developing world. The editor of a large denominational publishing house asked, "Dr. Haggai, how do you reconcile goal setting with the sovereignty of God? Is not goal setting a presumption on God's will?"

"How many children do you have?" I asked him.

"Three."

"May I assume your great passion is that they might give their lives to the Lord and live God-honoring, Christ-centered lives?"

"Of course."

"May I also assume that you and your dear wife are praying fervently, instructing the children, and creating the atmosphere in your home most conducive to leading them to such a spiritual commitment, while at the same time taking care not to pressure them? In other words, you want the decisions to be their own decisions. Am I correct in this?"

"Yes. Our great desire is that they may know the Lord."

"May it not be said, then, that you and your wife have set a goal, and that this goal relates to the salvation of your children? If that be true, do you think you are profaning the sovereignty of God? Within the parameters of God's sovereignty, He gives freedom for our choices."

---

*We are to set our goals with reference
to God's will as we understand it.*

We do not profane God's sovereignty by setting goals. Rather, we are to set our goals with reference to His will as we understand it. The goals then are the steps we take in carrying out the will of God!

The Living Bible paraphrases Proverbs 24:3-4, "Any enterprise is built by wise planning, becomes strong through common sense, and profits wonderfully by keeping abreast of the facts."

Summary

Vision lays the foundation of all leadership. The leader's vision requires a commitment to act: a mission. You implement vision and mission by means of specific, measurable goals.

The vision and mission remain constant. In contrast, you should review goals regularly—probably daily. When you review your goals, you should assess which have been accomplished. Examine those not completed, determine what corrective measures to take, and, if necessary, set revised or even new goals.

Establish effective goals. That means make them specific, measurable, attainable, and tangible. Don't build your goals on optimistic predictions of what other people will do. Rather, assume that others will underperform. At the same time, don't allow your predictability to contain your goals. I've never set a realistic goal in my life. As a result, I have been pushed into overperformance.

Write your goals out in detail, going over them repeatedly to ensure that they get you where you want to go. Replace any of your intangible goals with matching concrete goals that you can act upon and measure. Also, state your goals in positive terms that draw you forward. And never hesitate to adjust your goals in the light of changing circumstances.

Adopt goal setting as an ongoing discipline. You cannot do it once and then forget it, like getting an inoculation from the doctor. Today's persistent acceleration of change in people, places, processes, and ideas demands nothing less of the leader than assertive, clearly defined goal setting in every area.

DECIDE TO
PROVE LOVE WORKS

Don't let the word *love* fool you.

Love isn't a sentimental feeling conjured up by a Hallmark card. Rather, love is an action that characterizes the influential leader's every relationship.

Napoleon Bonaparte—who wielded more power than most—knew that power alone could not make leaders strong. He said, "Alexander, Caesar, Charlemagne, and I founded great empires. But upon what did the creations of our genius depend? Upon force. Jesus Christ alone founded His empire upon love, and to this very day millions would die for Him."

In his enduring book *Managing,* Harold Geneen makes an important distinction between a leader and a commander. The leader, he says, focuses on the people, whereas the commander focuses on the task. The leader shows consideration and love. The commander simply says, "I want this done, by this date, and if it is not done, then heads will roll!"[12]

---

*Too often we confuse leadership with
popularity, power, showmanship, or
wisdom in long-range planning.*

Most so-called leaders today do not lead people. W.C.H. Prentice said that too often we confuse leadership with popularity, power, showmanship, or wisdom in long-range planning. None of these can substitute for leadership that connects personally to others. Nor will any prove as effective.

Love Without Feelings

A world leader once came to visit me in my office. Having seen the work of Haggai Institute, he said, "Dr. Haggai, you must have great love for the developing world."

"If by that you mean that right now my veins are pulsating with deep emotion," I replied, "then the answer is no. At this moment, I feel no more emotional warmth toward the developing world than I do toward this desk. But you are right. I have great love for the developing world.

"I also have great love for my son, who died in his twenty-fifth year. As I talk with you, I feel no great emotion about him. If I begin to tell you some of the experiences we have had together as a family, I could easily begin to feel and display emotion. Either way, that makes no difference to the love I have for him. My love doesn't increase with emotion. Nor does it decrease without it!"

*Love is something you do
not something you feel.*

The leader looked at me wide-eyed. He finally grasped what I was saying: Love is something you *do* not something you *feel*.

Putting love in your decision making has nothing to do with your emotions. How you feel does not matter. The love consists in the decision itself, not in how you felt when you made the decision. I can feel sorry for victims of an earthquake, but a far better barometer of my concern for them is whether I support efforts to help them.

In the definition I gave earlier, love is *the outgoing of the totality of one's being to another in beneficence and help.* In other words, love requires a mind-set, an act of the will. You can love without feeling anything at all. In fact, love in leadership achieves more when unencumbered by emotions.

The ancient Greeks had a special word for this kind of love. They called it *agape. Agape* love means God-like love, in the sense that only God has the strength and perfection to practice it perfectly. Jesus made the word *agape* essentially a Christian word, haloed with a glory given it by God. Jesus used it to express His attitude toward *all* men and women.

Nobody can go on *feeling* love all the time. A continuous emotional high—as intense as the one we experience at the birth of a child, the start of a marriage relationship, or a victory on the sports field—would soon burn us up and destroy us. Neither the mind nor the body could handle it. *Agape* love may stir deep emotions, but it never relies on them. And when the emotions have subsided and gone away, *agape* love remains.

---

*Love means that no matter what anyone
does to humiliate, abuse, or injure you,
you work toward that person's highest good.*

Set yourself high standards. Love involves the totality of one's being. It involves unconquerable consideration, charitableness, and benevolence. It means that no matter what anyone does to humiliate, abuse, or injure you, you work toward that person's highest good. That amounts to a tough requirement—and one that few leaders can claim to fulfill.

Remember that love relates to real needs. Leaders can easily give people what they want, because this produces a short-term payoff. But the influential leader must think ahead and set goals that provide for the group's highest good, even if the group does not yet share his clarity of vision.

All parents understand the tension between wants and needs. Nothing brings a bigger short-term gratification than giving children what they want. But the undisciplined child, whose parents do not love him enough to say no when it matters, will fail to build character and will eventually come to grief. Good parenting forces you to take a long-term perspective. You put up with the tantrum because discipline ultimately delivers the gifts of inner strength, security, and belonging. These constitute the child's real needs, and the wise parent will plan to fulfill them.

Leading corporations may seem a million miles from being a parent, but the same principle applies. Without being patronizing, the influential leader makes decisions that meet the real needs of others, even though the measures this requires may seem unpalatable.

Love is *active,* never passive. It demands expression. Also, love is *transitive.* It demands an object. Love is unerringly practical. It serves and it sacrifices. And in doing so, it cultivates in others the motivation to work hard and reach goals.

"Not a Chunk of Money to Charity"

In 1976, entrepreneur Anita Roddick founded the British retail chain Body Shop. From the start, Roddick's vision dominated the firm. She believed in the value of close relationships, and this found expression in her decision making. Here are some of the things she decided:

- Despite its rapid expansion, she made sure she knew her employees by name.
- She held parties for her managers in her back garden.
- She made sure she visited every store in her chain at least once a year, to ask and answer questions from staff.
- She kept an open phone line so that anyone in the company could contact her.

Roddick also strove to ensure that the care extended beyond the company itself. Following the example of the first Body Shop, all outlets adopted a community care project, including hospitals, old people's homes, or disabled children's centers. Says Roddick: "It is not enough to vote a chunk of money to charity. What is important is to involve people in giving, sharing, and helping."

Business associates noticed.

"She's a very caring person," a franchisee of four London shops said. "And that feeling of caring sifts right through the company."

Is this kind of practical concern relevant to business? Apparently so. In ten years, Body Shop grew to 90 shops in the UK, with 196 more outlets in 30 countries. Over the same period it drew in a profit of more than five million pounds.

Don't Kid Yourself

Alone, no leader can generate constant, selfless, practical love any more than a power station can produce a constant stream of electricity without consuming fuel.

Leadership makes massive demands. It isolates you. By addressing real needs rather than felt needs, you sometimes incur hostility and resentment. In addition, leadership requires constant giving of time, of effort, of goodwill, even when these are not reciprocated.

Being an influential leader constantly drains your resources. Where will you go to refuel yourself?

People depend on you. They often lean on you. When things go badly they complain, and when things go well they don't always remember to credit you or say thanks. In short, being an influential leader constantly drains your resources. Where will you go to refuel yourself?

For now I want to note a key requirement: inner certainty that you are loved and valued. That does not come from the people you lead—or if it does, it comes only occasionally. Nevertheless, you must have that inner certainty if you are to endure in leadership.

In what remains one of the best books I have read on the topic, Denis Waitley, consulting psychologist to the National Aeronautics and Space Administration (NASA), says, "The first, best kept secret of total success is that we must feel love inside ourselves before we can give it to others." He then explains, "If there is no deep, internalized feeling of value inside of us, then we have nothing to give or to share with others."[13]

So where does this awareness of being valued come from?

The saying that "behind every successful man is a strong woman" has plenty of truth in it. Home and family provide powerful buttresses of support. So do friends. So do mentors. We all need advice, sounding boards, affirmation, understanding, people with whom we can relax and unwind. That explains why things going wrong at home impose massive stress.

All these are important. But, in my view, to give *agape* love in leadership you need something deeper than supportive relationships with other human beings—no matter how close.

To exercise love in leadership, you must yourself experience the love of God. In the end, nothing less will do.

You need a certainty that God loves you. Great visions, remember, are ultimately a gift from our Creator. And only that Creator provides the love you can always depend on. Even the best friends may finally desert you. Even your family members can fail to understand and support you. To exercise love in leadership, you must yourself experience the love of God. In the end, nothing less will do.

You may say, "I'm not religious. I don't need God." But whether we like it or not, we all have a spiritual side. We all have spiritual needs. And those needs must find satisfaction if we are to operate effectively as leaders—in business, in politics, or anywhere else.

You take care of your body by visiting the gym. Your spirit needs the same help. Only by understanding that God loves, forgives, and accepts you can you achieve a healthy self-esteem.

Paul the apostle talks about this in terms of the "fruit of the Spirit" in Galatians 5:22-23. It's a package deal, because he uses the word *fruit* in the singular. "The fruit of the Spirit is love, joy, peace, longsuffering, kindness, goodness, faithfulness, gentleness, self-control."

You might conclude that these behavioral fruits grow naturally from a relationship with God, and to an extent they do. They are consistent with a faith that is, at one and the same time, a person's highest vision and deepest choice. But keeping the tree fruitful requires a daily visionary decision.

Engstrom's Advice

Ted Engstrom, former president of World Vision International, wrote one of the all-time great books on relationship management, *The Fine Art of Friendship*.[14] In it he advises: "Emphasize the strengths and virtues of others, not their failings and weaknesses."

> *"Emphasize the strengths and virtues of others, not their failings and weaknesses."*

To illustrate this point, he tells the following story.

After three years of marriage, Joe's relationship with his wife had hit a crisis. He no longer thought of her as attractive or interesting. He considered her a poor housekeeper who was overweight, and he no longer wanted to live with her. Joe was so upset that he finally decided on divorce. Before he served her the papers, he made an appointment with a psychologist to find out how to make life as difficult as possible for his wife.

The psychologist listened to Joe's story and then gave this advice: "Well, Joe, I think I've got the perfect solution for you. Starting tonight when you get home, I want you to start treating your wife as if she were a goddess. That's right, a goddess. I want you to change your attitude toward her 180 degrees. Start doing everything in your power to please her. Listen intently to her when she talks about her problems, help around the house, take her out to dinner on weekends. I want you to pretend that she's the most wonderful person you have ever met. Then, after two months of this behavior, just pack your bags and leave. That should get to her!"

Joe thought this was a tremendous idea. He started treating his wife as if she were a goddess. He brought her breakfast in bed. He had flowers delivered to her for no apparent reason. He took her on two romantic weekend vacations. He read books to her at night, and he listened to her when she complained. It was incredible what Joe was doing for his wife. He kept it up for the full two months. After the allotted time, the psychologist gave Joe a call at work.

"Joe, how's it going?" he asked. "Did you file for divorce? Are you a happy bachelor once again?"

"Divorce?" asked Joe in amazement. "Are you kidding? I'm married to a goddess. I've never been happier in my life. I'd never leave my wife in a million years. In fact, I'm discovering new, wonderful things about her every single day. Divorce? Not on your life!"

Most people find it difficult to treat others considerately without feeling some affection first. They want the feelings to come first before they act. But leadership love works in reverse. You practice love first. And then, usually, some degree of friendship and affection will follow.

Engstrom suggests some useful lines of action for leaders who want to build relationships:

- *"We must decide to develop friendships in which we demand nothing in return."* By its very nature, love is unconditional. Otherwise it reveals itself not as love but as self-serving manipulation. Sadly, manipulation occurs more frequently than love in the behavior of many so-called leaders.

- *"It takes a conscious effort to nurture an authentic interest in others."* We have a natural tendency toward self-interest (which we should not confuse with healthy self-esteem). It therefore takes a conscious effort to love. "Each of us is a one-of-a-kind creation. Therefore, it will always take time—often a long time—to understand one another." Leaders are usually busy people. Yet one cannot avoid the fact that relationships build up slowly. You must make time for loving leadership to flourish.

- *"Commit yourself to learning how to listen."* Do you really listen to people, trying to understand what they are saying? Or do you just let the other person talk while you plan what you will say next? The one who loves listens with understanding.

- *"Simply be there to care, whether you know exactly what to do or not."* Sometimes you will not have all the answers. So love involves supporting others, letting them know they are valued, even when they are in a difficult situation and have no immediate way out.

- *"Always treat others as equals."* Just because you are in a position of leadership does not mean you are better than others. Leaders are susceptible to conceit. For that reason, they must refuse to rely on rank in relationships with others.

- *"Be generous with legitimate praise and encouragement."* Such words build up the self-esteem of others. Words of criticism and discouragement, however, kill enthusiasm and love in others.

- *"Make your friends Number One, preferring them above yourself."* Here again we see a clear difference between the leader who loves and the power holder who manipulates. The leader puts others first. The power holder seeks only personal advantage.

Visionary Decisions to Help You Prove Love Works

As psychologist Erich Fromm says in *The Art of Loving,*[15] the practice of love requires discipline, concentration, and patience. You must treat it as a supreme priority.

Unlike the mechanic who deals primarily with things or the mathematician who deals primarily with ideas, the leader deals with people. And people respond well, and give of their best, only when they know they are treated with love.

Demonstrate in your behavior how love works.
Reveal in your life and actions love's practice and benefits.

Attempting to motivate with threats not only undermines strong leadership but delivers poor results. For one thing, the behavior of the group often reflects the leader's behavior. If you seek effectiveness, live and work as a role model. Demonstrate in your behavior how love works. Reveal in your life and actions love's practice and benefits.

Resolve to make visionary decisions that reinforce and express the influential leader's determination to prove that love works in leadership.

1. Prove love works by inner contentment

Only love can keep a person cheerful in all circumstances. Love does not deliver a superficial sense of elation, but a deep-seated conviction that all is well.

In the modern world, with its emphasis on self-gratification, we are taught to believe that happiness and joy come only when we get what we want and our felt needs are fulfilled. Today's generation too often associates contentment with a new car, a bigger house, and more toys.

In truth, however, these things will never bring contentment. Addicts to things always want more. That explains why buying consumer goods locks us into a closed circle of dissatisfaction. No matter how much you possess, you will always feel the need to make just one more purchase before you reach a point of satisfaction.

If you don't have contentment now, buying will never answer your need. True contentment springs from the ability to put your own concerns second and to express love for others by giving.

Generous people are contented people.

2. Prove love works by flexibility

I once was privileged to spend three weeks in the company of an Asian leader. The government of South Korea invited him to become the national president after the Second World War. He turned the invitation down because he wanted to devote himself to leadership in the church. This man, Dr. Han Kyung Chik, has remained my most potent example in the art and skill of leadership.

I asked one of his deputies how Dr. Han responded to criticism.

The man replied, "I remember one time when Dr. Han proposed an initiative. In response, a session member made a savage attack on Dr. Han's judgment. Dr. Han wept. He said, 'Apparently I did not pray sufficiently before suggesting this. Forgive me. I shall pray more earnestly about this.' Within a year, the entire session saw the wisdom of Dr. Han's proposal and adopted it, although he never again brought it up."

That story speaks volumes about the power of love. Dr. Han could have insisted on his idea and dragged the others along with him. He refused to do it. And the fact that he refused, and took his colleague's criticisms so seriously, ultimately led to a sound, strong, and unanimous decision in favor of the very proposal Dr. Han had first put forward.

The loveless, self-centered power holder will try to get his way by creating factions, skillfully fomenting conflict, and keeping others off balance. This modus operandi defeats its stated purposes. By working for harmony, the influential leader may lose some votes, but ultimately he will take the organization in a direction that benefits everyone. He doesn't waste energy on paranoid efforts to exterminate criticism.

3. Prove love works by temper control

Another thing I learned from Dr. Han was, "When you lose your temper, you lose everything."

Leadership invites huge provocations. People blame you when things go wrong. You may miss crucial opportunities because somebody failed to heed your orders. Reverses and uncertainties can produce ongoing and almost unbearable pressure. Still, you gain nothing by letting your frustration boil over into anger with others.

---

*No matter what the provocation, the effective leader
will not stoop to respond with patronizing contempt
or brutal vindictiveness.*

Any leader can get angry. The effective leader controls his temper. No matter what the provocation, he or she will not stoop to respond with patronizing contempt or brutal vindictiveness. Love always advises patience.

Rich DeVos and Jay Van Andel, originators of Amway, had a sensible way of solving disagreements. They used a principle of veto—they could make no decision affecting the company on which they were not united.

When they did disagree on an important issue, they brought to their headquarters in Grand Rapids, Michigan, a solid and successful businessman they both had confidence in. He would arbitrate. They resolved the conflict and pressed on.

4. Prove love works by simple kindness

When I was a teenager, I listened to the spellbinding Walter A. Maier on the Lutheran Hour's "Bringing Christ to the Nations" broadcast. Sunday after Sunday I sat before the radio transfixed by the greatest radio preacher on earth. I scraped up two dollars and mailed them to him with a letter. I apologized for such a small offering but told him it was all I had. I assured him of my faithful "attendance" to his broadcast and of my fervent prayers for him and his ministry.

I was astonished a few days later when I received from him a two-page typewritten letter. It was no photocopied mass mailing. He had typed it himself—the typing errors proved it, for no secretary could have been that bad! He answered my letter in detail. He told me how important my gift was. He encouraged me. He shared some personal insights and anecdotes. He said that "every dollar reaches 1500 people with the Gospel through our program, so your gift will reach 3000 people!"

I said to myself, *When I get older, if anyone writes me, I shall be as kind as Dr. Maier has been to me.*

Maier's response expressed love through kindness. No wonder his leadership influenced millions across the world.

5. Prove love works by always choosing the good

Choosing the good means:

- Distinguishing clearly between good and evil
- Judging rightly when practical choices confront you
- Doing the right thing even when other people aren't observing your behavior
- Having increased thoughtfulness and sensitivity in dealing with all people

The ancient empires of Greece and Rome did not value goodness. Instead, the Greeks worshipped the intellect and the Romans worshipped power. Yet goodness underlies strong leadership. Leaders with strong moral character attract trust.

When you keep your promises, you set a pattern of behavior that assures others they can do business with you.

The leader who displays goodness will not force his standards on others. He will not engage in such counterproductive behavior, because he knows people do not respond well to being harried and criticized. At best, they adopt their superior's code of behavior as a way of currying favor and increasing their power. The good leader will lead by example, encouraging others to imitate his behavior and internalize it.

6. Prove love works by reliability

Do you stay true to your word, even in small matters? When you keep your promises, you set a pattern of behavior that assures others they can do business with you. Its essence lies in honoring commitments—to yourself, to others, to the organization, to your family, and, fundamentally, to God. Faithfulness characterizes the influential leader.

Ask some questions about the way you conduct yourself:

- Do you make promises you know you won't keep?
- Do you pay your bills on time?
- Do you turn up at the expected time for appointments?
- Do you stay on course with your long-term commitments?
- Is your word your bond?
- Do you do more than your duty?

The American motel magnate Cecil B. Day opposed everything false. He refused to alter verbal agreements at the closing of real estate transactions, even when the alterations were legally permissible and would profit him. That kind of faithfulness gets noticed.

People will not willingly follow an unreliable leader.
They want one who can be trusted.

People will not willingly follow an unreliable leader. They want one who can be trusted. This kind of love in the leader makes others desire to follow. Love accomplishes what neither fame nor force, muscle nor manipulation can attain.

Summary

Love is not a sentimental emotion but an act of the will in which a leader works toward the highest good of others.

Leadership by love works, because it deals with the practicalities of forming good relationships with those around you. Good sense urges every leader to infuse his leadership with love. It works in business and politics, in the professions and education, in the church and in the home.

But love makes demands. You cannot sustain the kind of giving that love demands unless you have a strong sense of personal security rooted in the love of others close to you, and particularly in the love of God.

In the end, love comes down to making visionary decisions. To develop inner contentment. To practice flexibility in driving toward your goals. To control your temper. To exhibit genuine kindness in your dealings with others. To have a reputation for choosing the good and for demonstrating total reliability.

Love makes leadership influential. The business organization can accommodate a limitless number of such leaders. As a leader, you have a wide-open opportunity to help set the course of this changing world in the right direction. In that, love constitutes one of your most powerful resources.

DECIDE TO BE HUMBLE AND RIGHT

James Riady breaks the mold of business leadership. One of six children in the Riady family, he serves as CEO of the Lippo Group of companies and deputy president of the Indonesia Chamber of Commerce.

Today, the Lippo Group owns 48 schools. They plan to build a university campus in Singapore that will eventually accommodate 35,000 students. They own four hospitals and are building fifteen more in the next five years, all in Indonesia. They have built two of Indonesia's tallest apartment buildings, one 52 and the other 42 floors. And they own the largest retail mall: 1.8 million square feet with underground parking for 5000 cars.

James Riady came to a relationship with Christ in 1990. All 15 people in his business inner circle are Christians. They meet once a week to resolve issues that cross business lines. James notes that he keeps his focus on the ten most important decisions that will impact the business each year—another discipline that enables him to release the business to his leadership team and shift his priorities to his charitable concerns.

Remarkably, every Thursday this member of Indonesia's business elite buys an economy class ticket and flies to another city in Indonesia for local outreach. He spends the night at the home of a low-income family and leads a Bible study on Friday mornings for whoever comes.

Why does he do this? Because he refuses to let the privileges of wealth cut him off from the real world in which most people have to get along on limited means. He has taken the visionary decision to practice humility.

Not for the Fainthearted

Lao-tzu, the ancient Chinese philosopher, made a wise observation about the successful leader:

- He does things without desire for control.
- He lives without thought for private ownership.
- He gives without the wish for return.
- Because he does not claim credit for himself, he always receives credit.

Influential leaders are willing to put this precept into practice.

For example, Abraham Lincoln once signed an order transferring certain regiments of the Union army. Edwin Stanton, the secretary of war, convinced that the president had made a serious blunder, refused to execute the order.

"Lincoln's a fool!" he roared.

> *"If Stanton said I am a fool, then I must be,*
> *for he is nearly always right."*

When Lincoln heard what Stanton had said, he replied, "If Stanton said I am a fool, then I must be, for he is nearly always right. I'll step over and see for myself."

Lincoln did just that. When Stanton convinced him the order was in error, Lincoln quietly withdrew it.

Lincoln was certainly humble. Was he "humble and right"? It's about as tough a test case as you could find. Operationally, Lincoln had made a poor decision, and Stanton, who was under Lincoln's command, stated this loudly and publicly.

On the face of it, "humble and right" would have meant Lincoln graciously deferring to Stanton even though he knew Stanton was in the wrong to refuse a command from his superior. Very often, influential leaders *are* right on operational matters—just because it's their job to keep one step ahead of everyone else.

But that's not what happened here. For Lincoln, being right didn't mean calling every situation accurately. He made mistakes, just like everyone else. Being right meant he separated his ego from his decision making and took the best advice available, even if that advice ran counter to his own assessment. He was humble. *And* he was right.

This partly explains Lincoln's greatness. He rose above sensitivity to the opinions of others. One could not offend him easily. He welcomed criticism. In this way, he demonstrated a strength that few leaders ever match.

If you hope to rise to your potential
as a leader, you'll do well to meet criticism
with tranquility and pleasantness.

Contrary to popular opinion, humility gives tensile strength to leadership. If you hope to rise to your potential as a leader, you'll do well to meet criticism with tranquility and pleasantness. This approach strengthens your spirit, gives added thrust to your work, and wins the respect of others.

Being "humble and right" does not reduce you to a mouse, burdened with a sense of your own inferiority. In his moral life, the influential leader may exhibit the courage of a lion and the strength of a giant. Yet he doesn't fool himself. He doesn't see others as greater or more powerful than he is. And he doesn't see himself as greater or more powerful than they. He keeps things in proportion.

This provides a useful check on pride and arrogance. The influential leader rejects aloofness. His followers see his manner as helpful and courteous. Without pretending self-sufficiency, he recognizes his own gifts, resources, and achievement. He has a confidence resting on the knowledge that he enjoys peace with himself and with God.

Most leaders have a ceremonial role to fill. The leader must meet and entertain visiting dignitaries. The leader represents his followers at official events. The leader gathers and receives honors on the group's behalf. So, when American officials in Washington welcome the prime minister of India, they signify, through their treatment of that one person, the respect America has for the country of India.

> *False humility rarely works because most people can detect pride within seconds.*

In such circumstances, a leader can quickly become egotistical and self-important. Humility demands constant self-discipline. As the English poet Samuel Taylor Coleridge said, "The devil's favorite sin is pride that apes humility."

Such false humility rarely works because most people can detect pride within seconds, no matter how hard you try to camouflage it. By contrast, influential leaders do not need to lean on their accomplishments to win other people's approval. They will give credit in exact measure, exactly where it is due. They neither inflate their own achievements nor loudly downplay them.

After an opera singer has thrilled an audience with a glorious recital, how could she say, "That was terrible singing and the applause was not deserved"? She accepts the applause of others. But she also recognizes the role others have played in her success. The parents who encouraged her talent. The teachers who honed it. The friends and professionals who have helped develop her career. The God who created the human voice.

It takes a lot of strength to walk in humility. In our natural state, like the disciples of Jesus, we feel a constant urge to measure ourselves against others. Of all the steps to visionary decision making, humility poses the hardest challenge.

Why Is Humility Important in Organizations?

Humility might seem like a luxury in business or political leadership—an attitude some top leaders can afford because they no longer need to prove themselves. But humility constitutes a key to influential leadership because it produces results.

Humility wins the respect of others

Humility enhances the influence of the leader because people follow more enthusiastically when they perceive the leader to have selfless and worthy motives. This has a practical result—the leader who acts with humility comes closer to achieving his objectives. Why? Because the objectives of leadership involve the highest good of the group, not the leader's self-aggrandizement. Humility allows the leader to feel fulfillment in seeing the group move toward the achievement of its purpose. Leaders lacking this quality soon lose credibility.

Humility fosters calmness

The business world, particularly, promotes competitiveness, frantic activity, confusion, uncertainty, worry, and fear. In that setting self-sufficiency appears a plus. Yet self-sufficiency does not give calmness and strength. Contrast the leaders whose humility lets them exhibit serenity, tranquility, and poise. They are neither self-conscious nor offended by criticism. They have too much on hand to give thought to offenses, real or imagined.

Take, for example, Haggai Institute alumna Dr. Eliane Felix, a pediatrician in Brazil's Mato Grosso. Every weekend this highly quali-fied woman flies out from the city to lead medical ministry in the Pantanal, a vast, poverty-stricken area that for half the year suffers extensive floods and can be accessed only by boat.

A group of visiting Americans some years ago included the writer John Grisham. Felix and her ministry clearly made an impact on him, because his subsequent novel, *The Testament,* includes a character called Rachel Lane who works as a medical missionary in the remote reaches of Brazil and who, just like Dr. Felix, is dedicated, strong, and self-effacing.

Humility generates progress

Too often superficial thinkers link humility with lethargy, apathy, indecision, and inactivity. Nothing could be further from the truth. Instead of limiting the leader, humility will enlarge his life. It will lead to learning, faith, and service.

Humility results in an enlargement of life because the humble person feels contentment where he is.

Because the humble leader makes no pretense of being self-sufficient or knowing all the answers, he draws insights from others. Humility does not lead to the shriveling and neglect of personhood. On the contrary, it opens the door to the expansion of personality and indi-viduality. Humility results in an enlargement of life because the humble person feels contentment where he is. This means he often performs better on the job and receives more genuine advancement.

Humility underpins success

The late Sir John Templeton, who led the financial world to move into the global arena, wrote a book titled *The Humble Approach.* On the many visits I had with him, both in Atlanta and in the Bahamas, he insisted that pride had no place in investments. He told me that he usually lost on 40 percent of his trades.

This world leader demonstrated the true strength of humility.

Veteran market watcher and Dow Theory expert Richard Russell often comments on the need for humility when trading. It doesn't matter how good your analysis, when the market goes against you, you can't win. Trying to force the trade, insisting that you must be right, can result in a heavy loss. You need humility.

In general, pretending that you know something—when in fact you know less than you should—creates a dangerous cover for ignorance and confusion. It raises a barrier to intellectual progress. The influential leader reacts like Isaac Newton, the man who discovered the force of gravity. Looking back on his younger years, Newton said, "The great ocean of truth lay all undiscovered before me."

Like scholarship, leadership requires openness not dogmatism. The man who knows everything learns nothing. Only a humble attitude sets the stage for the knowledge and know-how that lead to success.

Visionary Decisions to Help You Be Humble and Right

If you want to lose weight, you go on a diet. If you want to know more about history, you study books and listen to lectures. But how do you become more humble? People with humility do not *think* of themselves as humble. In fact, the moment you think that you are humble you will probably congratulate yourself and slip into self-conscious pride.

The moment you think that you are humble you will probably congratulate yourself and slip into self-conscious pride.

Humility requires concrete initiatives. Resolve to make visionary decisions to help you be "humble and right."

1. Be humble and right by focusing on action not attitude

In the chapter on goal setting, I discussed intangible goals. Achieving greater humility amounts to an intangible goal. You can get to it only by selecting concrete objectives that take you in the same direction. If you perform the action, the attitude will slowly follow.

I started this chapter with the story of James Riady. Here we find an accomplished businessman whose visionary decision making includes a regular commitment to immerse himself in activities many of his peers would deem inappropriate to his level in society. As far as I know, James Riady has never "tried to be more humble." Yet his decision making has achieved that goal.

Some years ago a businessman who had climbed to a top executive position with an international oil company came to the first Haggai Institute session. When he arrived at the airport, Ernest Watson, then dean of Haggai Institute, met him and went with him to the baggage claim area.

Being humble and right makes you willing
to go unrecognized, to keep quiet about your merits,
to bear slights, insults, and false
accusations for the sake of a higher purpose.

The oil company executive turned to Dr. Watson and said, "Where is the servant to carry my bag?" Without any reply, Dr. Watson, a man then 66 years old and a recognized world leader, smiled and picked up the bag himself.

On arrival at the hotel room, the gentleman complained, "There is only one glass in my room, and I need two." Patiently and without any rebuttal, Dr. Watson secured a second glass for him. During the sessions, that executive came to realize the power of humility, because he saw it expressed in action.

2. Be humble and right by rising above rivalry

One of the toughest requirements of humility is nonretaliation.

You will feel enormous pressure to fight back when hurt or insulted. But the influential leader steps back from insult and acts in the best interests of the aggressor. That may mean refusing to get into squabbles with other drivers when you're on the road. Or it may mean not allowing provocative behavior in the workplace to seduce you into conflict. Being humble and right makes you willing to go unrecognized, to keep quiet about your merits, to bear slights, insults, and false accusations for the sake of a higher purpose.

Similarly, the influential leader will never criticize others in a way that makes him appear superior, even by implication. People often ask leaders for advice. And all too often, leaders respond as though they know everything and pretend a global understanding they do not possess.

3. Be humble and right by helping with ordinary tasks

At the Last Supper no servant or slave arrived to wash the feet of the guests—a ritual as important then as wiping the dirt off one's shoes is today. Peter did not offer to do it, nor did John. Nobody wanted to do a servant's job.

So our Lord laid aside His outer garments and wrapped a towel around His waist. He then poured water into a basin and went from one apostle to another, washing their feet (see Luke 22:27; John 13:2-17).

Even unbelievers laud Jesus as the greatest leader who lived. Yet He repeatedly overturned our expectations of leadership with a humility that His contemporaries found shocking.

As I wrote at the start of this chapter, James Riady has taken this seriously. He knows that humility sets a striking example. He also knows that it helps keep human pride in check and therefore assists his own self-management.

4. Be humble and right by treating everyone as equal

Jesus showed His humility by welcoming the young and the marginalized. He showed appreciation for the smallest offering and the simplest service (see Matthew 10:42). And He didn't choose His disciples by going to the *Who's Who* of Palestine.

In fact, in 1 Corinthians 1:26 and 27, Paul says, "Not many wise according to the flesh, not many mighty, not many noble, are called. But God has chosen the foolish things of the world to put to shame the wise, and God has chosen the weak things of the world to put to shame the things which are mighty."

> *The influential leader respects everyone,*
> *no matter what their status.*

The influential leader respects everyone, no matter what their status. It's just good relationships management. And it also helps prevent real skills from being overlooked.

5. Be humble and right by addressing every area of life

You can't be humble and right in one area of your life without addressing all the others. So look at everything you do and ask yourself what visionary decisions you plan to take.

- *Socially,* being humble and right means putting the preferences of others before your own. Watch somebody else's choice of movie, not yours.

- *Intellectually,* being humble and right means taking other people's ideas and opinions seriously. Sometimes your ideas are not the best!

- *Financially,* being humble and right means prioritizing giving above spending on yourself. As John Wesley once put it, "Earn all you can and save all you can to give all you can for as long as you can."

- *Physically*, being humble and right means maintaining and optimizing your long-term health rather than punishing your body for short-term advantage. Getting enough rest constitutes a strategic choice.

6. Be humble and right by committing time to God

Actions count. They get noticed. They speak louder than words. In this respect, the influential leader communicates without ever having to open his mouth. He does not quarrel. He shows gentleness to all, not just to those who act politely toward him. He practices patience. He lovingly shares the truth.

---

*The first path to humility involves
making Christ the Lord of your life.*

The first path to humility, therefore, involves making Christ the Lord of your life. Although you are born again only once, you must constantly renew your commitment to yield yourself to the lordship of Christ because self-will constantly struggles to dethrone Christ and rule your life.

That requires a time-commitment.

Jesus frequently retired into remote privacy to pray, submitting Himself, the Son, to God the Father: "Now in the morning, having risen a long while before daylight, He went out and departed to a solitary place; and there He prayed" (Mark 1:35). After feeding the 5000, He told His disciples to get into a boat and go to the other side of the Sea of Galilee while He sent the people away. "And when He had sent them away, He departed to the mountain to pray" (Mark 6:46).

Obedience to Christ constitutes perhaps the greatest visionary decision for humility.

The Quiet Professor

Professor Eliseo Pajaro of Manila, Philippines, was an outstanding leader. From boyhood, Pajaro shone as a musical talent of exceptional promise. He developed into a man of charm, achievement, and spiritual depth. He earned his Ph.D. at the Eastman School of Music in Rochester, New York, and not long afterward attained full professorship at the University of the Philippines.

In 1959, Pajaro became the first Filipino to receive a grant from the Guggenheim Foundation for a year's study in the United States. During that time, he composed an opera, which won the Filipino Presidential Medal of Merit. Twice he received the Republic Cultural Heritage Award. His entire adult life was punctuated with honors.

Dr. Pajaro was an academic, a composer, a conductor, a performer, but above all, a leader with a permanent place in Filipino history, culture, music, and spirituality.

A year before his death, I attended a dinner meeting that included some of the elite of the Philippines: representatives of government, academia, the judiciary, the church, medicine, the media, and multinational businesspeople.

I was struck by the unobtrusive way Dr. Pajaro took a chair in the back row. People rushed to sit by him. His face, a marvelously open countenance, revealed his wholehearted response to every speaker. His wife, also a retired professor, and a Haggai Institute alumna, had a major part on the program. He beamed. Afterward, he was crowded by many of these celebrated leaders. They all wanted a word with him.

It would never have crossed Dr. Pajaro's mind to tell people he was humble. A humble man does not concentrate on his humility. When I congratulated him on his achievements, he thanked me. He didn't deny them, but he made it clear that God had so blessed him he must honor God with his talent. To use his gift for the glory of God was his quiet passion.

Eliseo Pajaro's influence endures long after his death, independent of any public relations program or publicity scheme. He had the humility of an influential leader.

Summary

Humility pervades the consciousness of the influential leader.

He deliberately puts himself in submission to others, and is helpful and courteous. He takes a visionary decision to recognize his need of others, yet without underestimating his own gifts, resources, and achievements. He knows that he is always right in the sense of having confidence in his own judgment. But he does not depend on having others constantly defer to him, and he accepts that being "right" may sometimes include embracing the wisdom of others in preference to his own opinion.

Influential leaders do not take the easy way out by assuming a false humility. The person with false humility deceives himself but he rarely deceives others, and most people instinctively dislike those who appear pompous, self-adulatory, and arrogant.

Though the word *humble* has misleading connotations, the influential leader finds that acting with humility results in greater respect, serenity, enlargement of life, and success. For that reason, influential leaders take a visionary decision to avoid elitism, intolerance, class distinction, and self-promotion. The keynote of humility reveals itself in a willingness to serve others. That embeds humility in concrete actions that you can plan, perform, and measure.

DECIDE TO
LIVE WITHOUT COMPROMISE

I n reading the lives of great men," wrote President Harry S. Truman, "I found that the first victory they won was over themselves...self-discipline with all of them came first."

In 1945, the same year Truman became president, some of the world's leading intellectuals crowded into a packed auditorium at Baylor University to hear a young man named Bron Clifford. University president Pat Neff, himself an outstanding orator and a former governor of Texas, had ordered the school bells switched off so Clifford would not feel time-bound. Clifford held the audience spellbound for two hours and fifteen minutes.

At the age of 25, young Clifford touched more lives, influenced more leaders, and set more attendance records than most speakers in American history. National leaders vied for his attention. He was tall, handsome, intelligent, and eloquent. Hollywood invited him to audition for a part in a major movie. In the 1940s his income was $10,000 a week—that would equal more than $200,000 a week in today's currency. It seemed as if he had everything.

Less than ten years after that meeting in Texas, Clifford was dying. He had left his wife with their two Down syndrome children. He was drinking. The surgeon Dr. Ernestine Smith had done exploratory surgery on Clifford. Knowing he was near the end, she asked her pastor to visit him. Carl E. Bates was appalled to find Clifford occupying a grubby room in a third-rate motel on the western edge of Amarillo, Texas. Cirrhosis had left him too sick to continue his last job, selling trucks for Plains Chevrolet.

Despite his enormous promise, Bron Clifford died unwept, unhonored, and unsung. He had amazing gifts. Yet he lacked the one quality vital for sustained leadership: the ability to live without compromise.

The Man Who Knew What He Wanted

Contrast with Bron Clifford the black agronomist George Washington Carver.

Carver too was an American. But he enjoyed none of Clifford's privileges. Born to slaves, as a boy he witnessed a racist mob beat the brains out of a black man and burn his body in the public square. Despite achieving exceptional high school grades, he was rejected by the president of Highland University with the words, "We don't take niggers."

Carver enrolled at Simpson College. His paintings of flowers won prizes at the World's Fair Columbian Exposition. His musical genius won him a scholarship to the Boston Conservatory of Music. But he chose to specialize in agricultural chemistry.

"I can serve my race better in agriculture," he said. "I want to help the man furthest down—the Negro—by teaching him how to help himself."

Declining a prestigious teaching position at Iowa College, he packed his suitcases and proceeded to Tuskegee Institute, where he dedicated his life to agricultural research that would benefit his community.

*George Washington Carver could have
been a millionaire. But he never
compromised his vision.*

The inventor Thomas Edison offered him a salary in six figures. A rubber company and a chemical firm offered him blank-check retainers to work for them. But Carver refused to shift from his mission. He stayed at Tuskegee for $1500 a year.

Carver could have been a millionaire. But he *never* compromised his vision. He has been called the "Wizard of Farm Chemistry" and remains one of the few Americans ever elected to a fellowship by the London Royal Society for the Encouragement of Arts, Manufactures and Commerce.

Living Without Compromise Isn't Abstinence

You will not read much about self-control in management textbooks. And yet compromise has damaged the life and prospects of numerous leaders.

> *Taking a visionary decision to reject compromise*
> *means putting your entire life under discipline.*

Self-control comes down to successful leadership of your own character. Most people think of it as mastering bad habits: smoking, quarreling, drug abuse, excessive drinking. But if you cannot control your whole self, you will never control the areas you perceive as "going wrong." Taking a visionary decision to reject compromise means putting your entire life under discipline.

The Greek word for self-control comes from a root word meaning "to grip" or "to take hold of." It describes the strength of the person who takes a firm hold of himself, who stays in full control of himself. It applies, for instance, to athletes, who prepare for great sporting events by carefully regulating all aspects of their lives—eating, sleeping, and exercise.

Aristotle used this same word to describe the "ability to restrain desire by reason…to be resolute and ever in readiness to endure natural want and pain." He further explained that the man with self-control still feels desire and may be seduced from the way of reason. But he keeps desire under restraint, like a large dog on a leash.

Leaders seeking self-control must avoid negativity. The person who continually says, "I must not do this, I must not do that," actually undermines himself by focusing on what he *doesn't* want to do. Thus he etches in his brain the very thing he wants to get away from. He should visualize future success not present failures.

Winners Have Self-Control

Self-control matters to leaders. Without it, the leader diminishes his effectiveness and loses the respect of his followers. With it, people view him as one who has admirable determination and strength.

The English Civil War brought together two opposing cavalry leaders of great skill and courage. But only one had self-control. In battle, Prince Rupert, a dashing and charismatic commander, led his men on a charge against the enemy pikes and guns. They broke the line successfully. But Prince Rupert, thinking the battle now all but over, continued riding so that he and his men could plunder the enemy camp. By the time he returned, he was shocked to find his army retreating in disarray.

On the other side of the battlefield, Oliver Cromwell had made a similar breakthrough. But Cromwell knew better than to give in to the craving for loot. As soon as he'd broken the enemy line, he rallied his men, turned, and assaulted the enemy infantry from behind. His self-control—and his ability to reproduce that self-control in his troops—brought him victory.

A battle fought 300 years ago may not seem the obvious model for modern leadership. But you will find exactly the same principle at work on the dealing floors of the world stock markets. The trader who remains focused and controlled, who refuses to let the passions of the moment divert him from his long-term goal, will always outperform a brilliant but undisciplined competitor.

Cromwell's success had another component. Long before he reached the battlefield, he insisted that his political masters make adequate funds available to the army. He insisted that his men receive proper food, adequate pay, and decent armaments. Prince Rupert used more old-fashioned and less reliable methods. And the difference showed.

The leader lives in the future.

Cromwell was a great leader because he could anticipate tomorrow's needs and meet them today. That is not easy. The effective leader has a clear vision of where his group will be three years hence. The leader lives in the future. With his top assistants, he actively plans programs that will accomplish and provide for that vision. But self-control may require that he make expenditures ahead of time and against today's priorities.

Leadership requires a cool head. While others respond to what they see, the influential leader responds to the real situation—the direction of the long-term trends.

Many businesses, for example, get into trouble by borrowing to expand in a booming economy. They overreach themselves, and then, when the bubble bursts, they find they are saddled with unrepayable debts. Resisting the temptation to cash in on short-term benefits marks out the influential leader. It takes self-control. It also takes—as Cromwell found on the battlefield—the skill of making others see that restraint pays bigger dividends.

The City Founder

Earlier I mentioned businessman James Riady. His father, Mochtar Riady, an ethnic Chinese Indonesian, always had his heart set on banking. Fifty years ago, Indonesians would not allow ethnic Chinese to work in prestigious positions. Riady never lost his focus nor weakened in his determination to go into the banking business.

While he was waiting, he began repairing bicycles. Then he sold bicycles. The day came when he was given a menial job in the bank. He worked fervently and faithfully, simultaneously pursuing his studies. He kept up this incredible pace until he earned a doctorate.

Finally he founded the now world-famous Lippo Bank and Lippo Insurance Company. He developed a multinational business that covered many areas of endeavor, including construction, real estate, education, and merchandising.

In a span of less than three years, he and his son James developed a 600-acre tract into a "city of tomorrow." Many global business analysts have considered Lippo City the most advanced in Asia. Some consider it the most advanced in the world.

Mochtar Riady made arrangements for his sons to receive the best possible education. He also gave them valuable practical experience by letting them work in financial, insurance, and property institutions.

More than once, he laid everything on the line and exposed himself to what could have been financial disaster.

Through it all, he treated people fairly and insured that they would enjoy value-added benefits by their alliance with his businesses.

When he bought the 600 acres, he saw to it that all the people in the area were provided better homes than they had previously known and employment opportunities previously denied them.

He built a 300-bed hospital, a four-star hotel, and housing that compare favorably with the upscale residential districts of any city on earth.

His sons developed great business capabilities and demonstrated unusual acumen, coupled with superior skills in handling business relationships.

On many occasions, Riady faced opposition. He experienced cruel betrayals. He never seemed to lose his upbeat, optimistic mindset. He controlled his feelings and thus controlled his environment. He did not allow his environment to control him.

During a period of unrest, caused by what many Indonesian citizens perceived as corruption, some unleashed their hostility on Riady. The damage to Lippo City amounted to millions of dollars. Yet I never heard him complain. He must have suffered profound grief when some of those he had emancipated from poverty started looting his stores and factories.

---

*Again and again, otherwise competent
leaders have courted destruction
through lack of self-control.*

During the 1990s, when politicians and pundits heaped opprobrium on the family, the Riadys simply put their confidence in God and waited patiently until the truth finally emerged.

Mochtar Riady demonstrates day by day the benefit of self-control.

How to Compromise—and Lose

Again and again, otherwise competent leaders have courted destruction through lack of self-control. It can occur in many areas:

- Some leaders allow greed and extravagance to influence them to embezzle money or cheat their organization.

- Some leaders have been lured by sexual temptations that destroy their family stability and credibility.

- Some leaders talk indiscreetly, costing other leaders the respect of their followers and resulting in the loss of confidential information.

- Some leaders give in to gluttony or alcohol abuse, destroying their careers and wrecking their health.

- Some leaders fall victim to pride and self-indulgence, losing their judgment and ability to make good decisions.

We tend to think of these as extreme situations that affect a few unwise individuals. In reality, however, all leaders are susceptible to them. Privilege and a sense of loneliness make leaders particularly vulnerable.

And these failures of self-control will put your leadership under pressure long before they actually destroy you. Most leaders do not embezzle large funds—but many are too liberal with their expense accounts. Most leaders are not gluttons—but many eat too much and exercise too little.

Self-control doesn't vanish overnight. It slips away little by little under the constant pressure of an unguarded lifestyle. Paradoxically, this erosion of self-control most often happens in those areas where you think you are strongest and feel most confident and secure.

Self-control doesn't vanish overnight. It slips away little by little under the constant pressure of an unguarded lifestyle.

When the leader does not have control over his own spirit, the smallest upsets will start to annoy him. The shabbiest allurements will start to draw him into the side alleys of leadership-destroying trivia. The smallest provocations will start to anger him.

Victimized by his own undisciplined passions, and making his neglect of self-control habitual, the leader loses finally the confidence of those he leads. He sinks into complete uselessness. And, tragically, this self-indulgent person makes himself the slave to those who are self-controlled.

Handling the High-Stress Decisions

Influential leaders will always resist the subtle pressures of the crowd.

John Templeton, Wall Street's most successful financier in the field of mutual funds, spent comparatively little time in New York City. He made his residence on the Bahama Islands because he wanted to do his own thinking without being swayed, however imperceptibly, by prevailing Wall Street wisdom. His consistent self-control explains why Templeton left such an impact on the financial world.

Self-control gives the leader courage to stand alone when others question his vision. The habit of self-control will teach a leader the importance of relying on his own evaluations rather than relying on popular opinion. Many leaders shiver at the thought of individual responsibility. They don't determine their stand until they first test the direction of the wind, consult a popular poll, or detect a consensus.

An attitude of self-control develops strong character. It never counts its companions. Nor does it judge itself by the number of its admirers.

The real test of a leader's courage and ability to stand alone comes in times of crisis.

The leader realizes the importance of standing alone because continuous contact with his followers weakens him. He will sink to their level. He will accommodate to their habits and fancies. Being part of the group offers more comfort than rising above the group. Yet only by rising above the group can the leader meet the group's highest needs and give it a vision that will result in changes of beneficial permanence. I don't mean you have to stand aloof, for aloofness will alienate your followers. But you do have to keep your own counsel and to spend time in solitude.

The real test of a leader's courage and ability to stand alone comes in times of crisis. When the stock price sinks. When the credit runs out. When people start to lose their nerve. A crisis removes all subterfuge, double-talk, and posturing. At such times, you must have self-control. If you don't, collapse will quickly follow.

Probably no foreigner has been more influential in Shaoxing, China, than Claude H. Barlow.

In the early twentieth century, as a doctor in China, Barlow came across a strange disease for which he knew no remedy. It was killing the people. At that time, no laboratories were available locally for research. Dr. Barlow filled his notebook with observations of the disease in hundreds of cases. Then, armed with a small vial of the disease germs, he sailed for the United States. Just before he arrived, he took the germs into his own body and then hurried to the Johns Hopkins University Hospital, where he had studied.

Claude Barlow was now a very sick man: He turned himself over to his former professors as a human guinea pig for their study and experimentation. A cure was found, and the young doctor recovered. He sailed back to China with scientific treatment for the scourge and saved a multitude of lives.

When asked about his experience, Dr. Barlow simply replied, "Anyone would have done the same thing. I happened to be in the position of vantage and had the chance to offer my body."

Not many would practice this kind of leadership, nor does the business world afford much opportunity for it. But Barlow's self-control stands out. Given his goal to provide excellence in medical care, he was willing to take an extraordinary risk for the sake of finding the necessary cure. No wonder his leadership had such a profound impact when he returned to Shaoxing.

Such leadership will draw the followers to the leader and establish him as influential.

Visionary Decisions to Help You Live Without Compromise

As with learning any skill, self-control requires commitment and practice. At no time in his life will the leader enjoy freedom from temptation. Some desires are more urgent in the young. Others peculiarly afflict the old. The need for self-control never goes away. So how do you strengthen and develop it? Resolve to make these visionary decisions to help you live without compromise.

1. Live without compromise by conscious dependence on God

Says Richard Foster: "Will-power has no defense against the careless word, the unguarded moment. The will has the same deficiency as the law—it can deal only with externals. It is not sufficient to bring about the necessary transformation of the inner spirit."[16]

Here again you cannot separate the practicalities of leadership from deeper things. The exercise of self-control ultimately depends on something outside of your own mind and heart. A leader who lacks this perspective, and this readiness to admit that he or she must rely on and defer to a superior spiritual force, will never achieve true self-control.

2. Live without compromise by submitting yourself to discipline

A life characterized by self-control begins with an attitude of discipline. Regular exercise takes discipline. Maintaining an organized workplace takes discipline. Getting out of bed on time takes discipline. You need discipline to have a healthy diet.

Those who are disciplined in small things tend to be disciplined in big things as well.

You may think the small things don't matter, but those who are disciplined in small things tend to be disciplined in big things as well. By contrast, those who lack discipline in minor details will lack discipline everywhere.

In an age increasingly geared to consumption, discipline has become increasingly rare. People see it as too demanding, too high-minded, too perfectionist. Yet discipline—including a basic religious discipline—pays enormous dividends in leadership. Mediocre leaders make compromises and give themselves the luxury of little self-indulgences. Influential leaders—from Rockefeller to Gandhi to Mandela—all made discipline a lifestyle priority.

3. Live without compromise by making decisions in advance

When Daniel, Shadrach, Meshach, and Abed-Nego were chosen for special training in Babylon, they purposed in their hearts that they would not defile themselves "with the portion of the king's delicacies, nor with the wine which he drank" (Daniel 1:8).

Thus when they were actually faced with the opportunity to eat the king's food and drink the king's drink, they didn't have to make a decision under pressure. They had already made up their minds. They knew they wouldn't do it.

Self-control becomes easier when you purpose in your heart how you will act in certain situations.

Self-control works best when you make your decisions ahead of time—and live according to those decisions.

Long ago I made the visionary decision to correct overpayment. If I buy a three-dollar item with a five-dollar bill, I don't have to think twice about returning the extra money if I receive seven dollars in change. It's automatic. I don't give myself the opportunity to rationalize that "the store charges too much for its goods and so the error simply evens things out."

Self-control works best when you make your decisions ahead of time—and live according to those decisions. In effect, you are writing your rules for living. Writing and internalizing such rules not only strengthens your leadership, but also gives you greater self-confidence and serenity. Having the power of habit on your side confers great advantage.

4. Live without compromise by taking responsibility

A friend told me that he could not possibly control his temper. He attributed his ungovernable explosions of anger to his parents and grandparents. He said that no one could ask a person like him to rule his own spirit.

I asked him, "If you were in a heated argument with your wife, and someone knocked on your door, would you continue to shout?"

He had no answer. Saying he was incapable of self-control was simply an excuse. The real problem was his unwillingness to address his antisocial behavior. He really could control his temper—when he wanted to. He simply hadn't got into the habit of ruling his spirit. He had never taken responsibility for it.

In exercising self-control, you must learn to take all sorts of abuse without retaliation. When an angry person starts to vilify and abuse you—justly or unjustly—you must remember that retaliating only draws you down to that person's level. When that happens, you forfeit your leadership, for you have allowed somebody else to control your emotions instead of controlling them yourself.

Ponder the wise saying: "He who is slow to anger is better than the mighty, and he who rules his spirit than he who takes a city."[17]

5. Live without compromise by thought-control

The influential leader realizes that self-control really comes down to thought-control. Consequently, he insists on doing his own thinking. Thinking about your vision, your mission, your goals, and the needs of your group several times daily—especially upon awaking and before retiring—will go a long way toward guaranteeing your exercise of self-control.

Thinking about your vision, your mission, your goals, and the needs of your group several times daily will go a long way toward guaranteeing your exercise of self-control.

Picture the way you will act as a leader characterized by self-control. How will you react to people in various situations? How will self-control contribute to your goals and mission? Picture your group as you see it one year and three years from now. Putting these images clearly in your thoughts will help you act them out in reality.

Also, reflect in detail on situations where you have already demonstrated self-control. Athletes train in this way. They learn to relax and visualize their best performance—how they felt, what they heard, odors they noticed, the taste of the water or dirt or air. They are told to input all of these sensory-rich impressions into their brain so next time they can perform even better. Big league sales people and notable orators have been doing this for years.

Develop your self-control by taking time each day, preferably early in the morning or late at night, to remember your victories—the times you achieved self-control when the normal response would have been anger, fear, or intimidation.

You have the ability to make your thoughts do your bidding. Only two impulses set your brain in motion: your own will or stimulus from outside. Examine yourself. It will shock you how often pressure from others—deliberate or otherwise—provokes you into a response you would not otherwise have made.

You have the power to determine what you think about. Act on this ability. Deliberately choose the thoughts you want to dominate your mind.

You are the product of your thoughts. Yet you have the power to determine what you think about. Act on this ability. Deliberately choose the thoughts you want to dominate your mind. Decisively deny admittance to all outside suggestions that don't square with your values and commitments. It will develop your self-control and enable you to influence others instead of having others influence you.

6. Live without compromise by practicing thankfulness

It fascinates me that, of all the New Testament writers, only Paul used the word *adversity*. Adversity was his constant Spirit-administered discipline. He could have become bitter about his adversities, but he rejoiced in them because he knew they were given for his benefit. He could finally say, "I take pleasure in infirmities, in reproaches, in needs, in persecutions, in distresses" (2 Corinthians 12:10).

At the peak of his career, God sent Paul a "thorn in the flesh" to buffet him lest he be "exalted above measure." What a blessing!

God had equipped Paul with gifts of character, energy, and power. He possessed the capacity to command, to lead, to organize. His was a great mind that could articulate the truths of God to both the literati and the illiterate. However, had it not been for the presence of his infirmity, he may never have achieved for God such splendid work. He may have surrendered to self-centered confidence rather than developing self-control. He may have relied upon his extraordinary endowments instead of casting himself completely on the power of God.

Scripture assures us that suffering produces joy and "the testing of your faith produces patience" (James 1:3). Adversity is God's refining fire. In the crucible of suffering you have the greatest opportunity to develop and exercise self-control. During Job's suffering, his wife urged him to "curse God and die." Job responded, "Though He slay me, yet will I trust Him" (Job 2:9; 13:15).

*You should show gratitude for those experiences
God gives you that will build self-control.*

That kind of self-control comes as the result of adversity. You should show gratitude for those experiences God gives you that will build self-control. He gives you those experiences because He loves you and wants to see you develop love so demonstrated through self-control.

The Three Benefits of Self-Control in Leadership

When you refuse to compromise, you set up the psychological conditions for realizing your vision. You avoid distractions. And you no longer tolerate elements of your own behavior that contradict your overall objectives.

So don't make the mistake of thinking of self-control as a form of *limitation*. In fact, it represents self-mastery springing from love. Discipline does not produce a harsh, joyless existence. Rather the opposite: it produces a well-balanced personality with the following characteristics.

Freedom

Self-control produces freedom through bringing self-centeredness and fear into subjection. Self-control cuts down on nagging decisions about whether you should indulge private vices and avoid public duties. You have already made up your mind. You don't have to struggle with the decision. The freedom produced by self-control comes from knowing you have mastered your habits instead of letting them master you.

*The freedom produced by self-control comes from
knowing you have mastered your habits instead of
letting them master you.*

You need to experience this freedom to appreciate it. The commercials tell you repeatedly that freedom comes not from self-control but from self-indulgence—the next holiday, the next expensive dress, the next drink. In reality, unrestrained self-indulgence leads to slavery, both financial and spiritual.

Paradoxically, freedom rests on laws that limit and define actions. This applies in natural science. For example, a stone can obey only one law: the law of gravity. Consequently, it remains motionless and inert. A worm can obey two laws: the law of gravity and the law of motion. It can rest quietly, but it can also move by its own volition. A bird can obey three laws: the law of gravity, the law of motion, and the law of aerodynamics. It can rest, it can walk on the ground, and it can fly.

Self-discipline produces freedom by shutting off useless options. You may choose to drive on the left side of the road in the U.S., but it won't do you any good and will likely lead to harm. Only when you obey the directive to drive on the right do you have the freedom to reach your destination quickly and safely.

Consider the river directed to great turbines at the edge of the city. Using the water's power, the turbines light and heat the city's buildings. If banks do not confine and control the river's flow, the turbines will not move, and the power will fail. Once again, limitation produces freedom.

Confidence

When I was a young man, I spent some time in the company of the late Robert G. LeTourneau, builder of the world's largest earth-moving machinery. He once said to me, "John, it's all in the mind."

"Yes, sir," I replied. "What's in the mind?"

"Money," he said.

"Would you please explain that to me, sir?"

"Well, let's suppose that a rumor got out that all the gold in Fort Knox, where America keeps its gold bullion, had disappeared, even though the gold was still there. What would happen?"

"People would go into panic. There would be a run on the banks."

"Exactly. On the other hand, suppose that all the gold were to disappear, but nobody knew about it. What then would happen?"

"Nothing. Commerce would go on as usual."

"Exactly. That's what I mean. It's all in the mind."

Self-control is a form of success from which
further confidence naturally springs.

The very wheels of commerce move forward on the attitude of confidence. Those who play the stock markets confidently, on the basis of sound insight, generally come out the winners. Self-control produces a confidence and assurance that you are capable of leadership. If you can regulate your own desires, you can rely on your own future performance in leadership. Your leadership practice will conform to the principles you endorse as right. Self-control is a form of success from which further confidence naturally springs.

Stability

Few people like change. We want things to stay the way they are. People look to leaders who will provide them with stability. A disciplined life does not remove change, but it does mean that the change will have purpose. Self-control produces stability.

In 1933, when Franklin Delano Roosevelt became president of the United States, the nation was in the throes of its worst ever economic depression. The unemployment rate had topped 25 percent. Men who had been millionaires one day were selling apples on the street corner the next. They had traded in millions; now they were scraping to make a few pennies. President Roosevelt got on the radio and calmed the fears of the American people with these words: "We have nothing to fear but fear itself."

Roosevelt's own confidence and stability played a key role in gaining the confidence of the American people and starting the nation on the long road back to prosperity.

Summary

Refusing to compromise constitutes a way of life. By living a controlled life, the leader prevents desires from mastering him. He keeps himself free from the craving for short-term gratification that often obstructs long-term goals. The leader who exercises self-control rarely tastes defeat. In contrast, the person who cannot control himself ultimately becomes the slave of the person who can.

Lack of self-control destroys leadership. The leader needs to take particular care. Loss of self-control often begins in areas where he demonstrates strength, has the most confidence, and feels the most secure.

Self-control gives courage to stand alone—a vital asset in leadership. It allows the leader to concentrate on his vision and to resist the subtle pressure to conform to the crowd. Self-control allows influence to move the other way. The influential leader stands apart from his group in order to exert an influence over them. Maintaining that distance requires a refusal to compromise.

Like all the principles of leadership, self-control requires careful nurturing. This requires a recognition of powers that stand above you. It also requires a life of discipline, a readiness to make decisions ahead of time, a willingness to take responsibility, and a resolute control of your thoughts.

Some see self-control as a restriction, a discipline that saps life of its pleasures. In reality, the opposite applies. Self-control is one of the core qualities of leadership, carrying enormous personal benefits for the influential leader.

DECIDE TO
PERSUADE AND WIN

One of the most in-depth studies on persuasion was made by two professors of New York University's speech department, Alvin C. Busse and Richard C. Borden.[18] These two indefatigable researchers spent seven years listening to no fewer than 10,000 arguments. They included in the study everything from domestic disputes and wrangles between taxi drivers to debates in the United Nations. Major companies such as Macy's and Westinghouse allowed them to observe their salespeople and counter clerks in action.

Their goal: to find out who won the argument—and why.

Half a century later, what Busse and Borden found out remains fundamental to the business of persuasion.

Battering someone else's argument to the ground is likely to get you the opposite of what you want, because nobody likes to lose.

They discovered that in getting ideas accepted, professional debaters—including politicians—came in a poor second to door-to-door salespeople. The reason: unlike the politicians, the lowly salespeople had no interest in scoring points or dismantling the opposition's argument. Ego had nothing to do with it. They aimed simply *to induce the prospect to change his own mind.*

It pays to remember that people have minds of their own, and that they are much more likely to change their own minds than have someone do it for them. In fact, battering someone else's argument to the ground is likely to get you the opposite of what you want, because nobody likes to lose.

People on the receiving end of "the truth" may have all sorts of reasons for not accepting it. The medical patient may be in denial over an alarming diagnosis. The executive may have locked himself into his own program or plan. The teenager may care more about the opinions of her peers than those of her parents. In each case, careful explanations and faultless logic will fall on deaf ears. The person just doesn't *want* to know.

---

*In the end you don't win arguments;
you win hearts.*

For this reason, enter intellectual battles reluctantly and with caution. The influential leader will learn fast to rely not just on compelling reason but also on clearing the way for others to change position. In the end you don't win arguments; you win hearts. And that's quite a different thing.

The Smartest Thing You'll Ever Do

If you want to persuade, start by listening.

Listening has become a hugely underrated skill. Advertisers and salespeople have amassed formidable expertise in reading audience demographics. Market researchers devise ingenious ways of extracting information from the public and turning it into tables and charts.

Agents in the security services spend thousands of hours reviewing phone tap recordings.

All of them gather information; none is listening.

Listening involves paying sympathetic attention to another person and understanding what makes him or her tick.

Too many leaders make the mistake of thinking their influence lies in keeping the initiative and making a lot of noise. Such a leader will impress at first, but over the long haul will not inspire confidence or loyalty. Influential leaders listen.

You can witness the power of listening every time someone you admire pauses to ask your opinion. You cannot help but feel a little flattered. For a few moments you stand in the spotlight as an expert. Consciously or unconsciously, the bond between you and the person you admire receives an extra layer of strength.

Influential leaders listen.

Influential leaders know that others like to be helpful, like to contribute, like to play an important role. In short, they love to be asked.

Influential leaders also know that, once they get another person talking, all kinds of information will come out. Not just what the person says, but what he leaves out, what manner and tone of voice he uses, what attitude he strikes, what loyalties and opinions he betrays.

Persuasion in the Team

Lowell Thomas was arguably America's premier explorer during the early part of the twentieth century. He made a fortune speaking to live audiences. He also presented the longest running newscast in American history up to that time.

I knew Lowell Thomas well. He told me that his college courses in public speaking were more important than all his other courses combined. He said, "If I had to choose between taking only the courses in communication and taking all the rest, I would not hesitate—I would take the courses on communication."

If you want your vision to be realized, you will need other people to help. The company, not the owner, constructs and sells the product. The team, not the coach, plays the game and wins the trophy. The army, not the general, achieves victory in battle. For this reason, a leader must be able to communicate vision, mission, and goals effectively to his followers. He must be a communicator.

> *A leader must be able to communicate*
> *vision, mission, and goals effectively.*
> *He must be a communicator.*

Effective communication within your group delivers further benefits.

Effective communication brings a group together.

Members of a group can be isolated from each other by geography, language differences, or attitudes such as class distinction, religious sectarianism, racial segregation, nationalism, or political partisanship. Such division frustrates group achievement. Through effective communication, the leader can encourage the kind of understanding, tolerance, and sympathy that will bring isolated members into unity with the rest of the group.

Only by effective communication can a leader cultivate leadership skills in others.

Almost 200 years ago, British statesman Samuel Morley said, "He who does the work is not so profitably employed as he who multiplies the doers." The phrase deserves study.

"No man ever began a movement which was destined to stand the test of time but that he placed great stress on the task of teaching those who followed after him," said Dr. Herschel H. Hobbs, former president of the Southern Baptist Convention. "Leaders may come and go, personalities may live and die, but mental and spiritual concepts are immortal. These are the dynamics for changing the course of history and the lives of men and women."[19]

No leader can succeed without this power to reproduce great thoughts, beliefs, and ideas in others. Unfortunately, most communication in business falls far short of its aims. The chief executive of a company may have a clear vision for the company's future. But the workers will often distrust his motives and so perpetuate that fatal split between management and labor.

Similar things happen in other professions. The professor seeks to impart vital knowledge—but leaves the students confused. The lawyer pleads earnestly before the jury—but he loses the case. The salesman extols his superb products—but he makes no sales. The father wisely counsels his son—but the son shows no change in attitude or action. The political leader presents strong policies to the crowd—but fails to win the election.

The ability to be persuasive,
through speech and writing, is possibly
the leader's most valuable asset.

Communication is the means by which we transfer truth. Communication can move and mold others, individually and collectively. The ability to be persuasive, through speech and writing, is possibly the leader's most valuable asset.

It also frequently goes wrong.

Don't Assume Your Message Gets Across

You are at the airport catching a plane for a lunchtime meeting in New York. When you check your messages, you find out that the Japanese delegation scheduled to arrive tomorrow has been rerouted in Madrid and will now be arriving this afternoon. It's imperative that somebody of appropriate rank meets them in person and conducts them to their accommodations—the booking for which now has to be brought forward by 24 hours.

Immediately you call your personal assistant, but she doesn't pick up. It's only 8:15 a.m.; probably she's driving and has her cell phone switched off. So you leave a brief message explaining what you want her to do and telling her you'll call from New York.

For the next three hours you're in the air.

Business offices the world over exhibit communication problems that can seriously undermine competitive advantage.

At midday you're about to call her again from a taxi when you get a text message telling you her daughter has been in a car accident. She's left all business with Suzie, her No. 2, while she goes to the hospital. You have five minutes before you start your afternoon meeting. Suzie's line is busy, so you call Gene, your head of sales, who's great at talking but poor at logistics, and tell him to stand in for you as host for the delegation and to brief Suzie on rebooking the hotel.

Gene tells you "I'm on it," which makes you feel good, but when you call again at three you get his voice mail.

At that point a number of questions occur to you about the communication process:

- Did you think out clearly what you wanted to say to Gene, or were you improvising?

- Did you include every pertinent detail?
- Was the line clear enough for him to hear everything you said?
- Was he taking notes?
- Does he really understand the urgency of the situation, and will he prioritize it over his own workflow this afternoon?
- What will he do if he cannot reach Suzie?
- What will Suzie do if she runs into problems with the hotel booking?
- Why did you forget to ask Gene which hospital your PA's daughter is in so you can order flowers?

We communicate every day. But we also miscommunicate every day. Meanings get garbled, mixed up, misinterpreted, lost. And clearly much hangs on getting it right. You will insult your Japanese guests if you fail to meet them at the airport. If you fail to establish a good relationship with the delegation, your business will suffer. Communication is already at the center of the whole process, and we haven't even touched on the minefield of communicating successfully across cultural boundaries.

Business offices the world over exhibit communication problems that can seriously undermine competitive advantage. The whole process of "encoding" meaning in verbal or written form (and then "decoding" it again) is fraught with difficulties, even if the two people involved know one another well and use the same language in more or less the same way.

Effective communication is both an art and a science. As an art, it requires the same earnest attention, persistent practice, and careful technique as the mastery of painting, sculpture, or music. As a science, it is based on the principles of psychology.

*The influential leader prepares his written
and verbal communication as thoroughly as
the conductor prepares his orchestra.*

The influential leader leaves nothing to chance. He prepares his written and verbal communication as thoroughly as the conductor prepares his orchestra. It is not enough to have great thoughts. Those thoughts must be communicated with power. Fail to overcome the problems of communication, and you will never reach your leadership potential.

Persuasion for Speakers

A student of John Knox recalled the great Scottish reformer preaching his last sermon. He wrote: "He made me so to tremble that I could not hold my pen to write. He was very weak...but before he had done with his sermon, he was so active and vigorous, that he was like to ding the pulpit to blads, and fly out of it."

Four centuries later, it's easy to picture the scene. It reminds me of advice given to me years ago by the preacher C.E. Autrey: "John, people don't come to hear what you say, they come to watch you burn."

*The trick isn't volume or histrionics; it's passion. An
influential leader will let the passion show.*

You don't have to shout to achieve this. Winston Churchill, widely acknowledged as one of the twentieth century's great orators, had a low-key, even monotonous style. Franklin Delano Roosevelt, who delivered some of his greatest speeches in radio "fireside chats," nevertheless galvanized the nation.

The trick isn't volume or histrionics; it's passion. An influential leader will let the passion show—the constant inner passion that arises from pursuit of a vision. People feel passion in the voice and the manner. They can see it in the eyes and the body language.

You can't teach people to be passionate any more than you can teach them how to fall in love. But when a leader reveals passion, others catch it. That is why the ability to speak effectively remains one of the greatest assets of leadership, and why passionate leaders enjoy such success.

When you speak, think out carefully what you want to achieve with your audience. In general your goals will include some or all of the following:

- *To inform.* This is the goal of all who seek to convey information purely as information. When a coach outlines a strategy for the game, his primary goal is to create understanding. He knows he has done this successfully if the team plays according to his plan.

- *To impress.* Besides imparting information, a speaker will often wish to move his audience emotionally—to pity, indignation, or desire. The lecturer on Kahlil Gibran will want his students not just to absorb the facts about the man but to feel admiration. The motivational speaker or the sales team leader will want the audience to leave not merely informed but filled with can-do.

- *To convince.* When he promotes an action plan for world poverty, the leader's goal is to convince—of the facts, of the importance of the facts, and of the effectiveness of the action proposed. He wishes each of his hearers to say, in effect, "You are right." The response looked for is cerebral, a shifting of opinion.

- *To entertain.* Many speakers fail for want of the ability to entertain. If you are a stand-up comedian, entertainment will be your first and probably your only goal. But you entertain also by having a good opening, a lively manner, and an interesting story to tell.

- *To actuate.* Any sales-related address will aim to make the audience take a specific action after the speech is over—to go, to give, to bring, to join, to do. To actuate is the main concern of the trial lawyer and the electoral candidate. If your hearers do not take the action you urge on them, you have failed to communicate no matter how well you have informed, impressed, convinced, or entertained.

You will struggle to achieve any of these goals, however, without analyzing your audience carefully.

On speaking tours, I used to arrive in town early and talk to some of the key personnel—the city leaders, a school principal, a union leader, a factory representative, the president of a high school student body. Choose the right contacts and you will get a reasonably accurate picture of the way people in your audience think.

Sometimes I got the basics wrong—and paid for it. During a speech in Australia, I made an impassioned plea for each person to vote during an upcoming election. I was trying to impress on my audience the importance of utilizing this precious privilege of a free society. Only after the meeting did I learn that voting in Australia was compulsory!

You must habitually ask yourself, "How would I feel about this if I were in the audience?"

Analysis should enable you to position yourself appropriately in relation to your audience by seeing things from their viewpoint. You must habitually ask yourself, "How would I feel about this if I were in the audience? Would I understand this point with the background they have? Would this sound reasonable if I had been through their experiences? Would it be interesting to me if I were in their position?"

This will help you discover common ground. Always refer to things that members of your audience have seen, heard, read, felt, believed, or done—things that linger in the listener's consciousness and his inventory of knowledge, including history and current affairs. Common experiences in these areas will deepen your credibility.

The best stories either refer to recent events or involve pain. Visiting Tehran, I was doubled over by the pain of a kidney stone. When I tell that story, I can be sure that everyone pays attention, because most can recollect a similar pain of their own. Similarly, though a war veteran may have served 50 years ago, the memories of that experience will remain intense.

Audiences will not be commanded, threatened, or maneuvered into an opinion.

Develop a repertoire of vivid experiences common to the average person. Impress these experiences on your mind. Audiences will not be commanded, threatened, or maneuvered into an opinion. They say, "I am a person. I have as much right to an opinion as you. Bring your thought in line with my mindset, and I may join with you."

You must always ask yourself, *What references to the listeners' experience will make my idea vivid to them? What will cause them to say, "I understand," "I empathize," "I agree," "I will do it," and "I am pleased"?* Answer that, and you will know what arguments come closest to the lives of your listeners and which appeals are most likely to move them.

You can succeed in the most unlikely situations.

I once spoke at Hockaday, an elite girls' school in Dallas, Texas. The officials warned me that the last several speakers had been interrupted. The girls would hum on one note, causing a distraction that made continuation of the speech impossible.

I told them I thought we would get along just fine. Within 15 seconds, using humor, I had captured their attention. Half an hour later they gave me a standing ovation. I was actually able to say every-thing that was on my heart. To this day, I receive letters from some of them—now mothers and career women—telling me of the impact that speech made.

Visionary Decisions to Help You Persuade and Win

Once a stranger in America stopped a man on the road and asked him, "Where does this road lead to?"

"Where do you want to go?" the man said.

Again the stranger persisted, "Where does this road lead to?"

"My friend, this road leads to any place in the United States."

It is the same with persuasion. Unless you have a clear plan, you will probably not succeed in drawing others around you in pursuit of your mission.

1. Persuade and win by working at conversation

When John F. Kennedy visited West Berlin during the Cold War—a Western island adrizft in the Soviet bloc—he began his address with four words of German: *Ich bin ein Berliner ("I am a Berliner")*. In little more than three seconds he had the entire crowd in the palm of his hand.

Communicating empathy and establishing common ground form the basics of successful persuasion, whether from a podium or one-on-one.

Listening impresses far more than speaking.

Poor conversationalists think of conversations as a tennis match. They hit the ball over the net, wait for it to come back, then hit it again. If they have very poor conversational skills, they'll barely listen to the other person; instead they'll be thinking about what they're going to say next.

Listening impresses far more than speaking—and also provides valuable information. So master the skills of listening by consciously focusing on the person who's speaking to you.

Start by actually looking directly at the person. If you look over his shoulder, he will think something is happening behind him. Stare at his tie and he'll think he's spilled coffee on it. So look him in the eye. And give affirmative signals by nodding and smiling in the right places.

Next, reply in the right way at the right time. Don't be too eager to butt in with a story you've just thought of or a contrary opinion. Hear the speaker out. Then follow up with a question. The other person will feel complimented if you say, "Tell me more about so and so" or "So you mean to say that…" In replying, repeat the actual words and phrases he has used, as this will help to embed them in your memory and reinforce that you have paid attention.

Find connections between the other person's position and your own.

All this gives you time to find connections between the other person's position and your own. Even if you disagree with what he's said, or cannot act on his suggestions, avoid blunt rebuttals or denials. Use formulas such as "I agree with you about…" or "As you were saying…" as this will establish common ground and make it far easier for the other person to move toward your point of view.

2. Persuade and win by breaking the preoccupation barrier

In the early 1970s, I addressed a meeting in the U.S.A. Though I knew little about the audience, I learned they'd been discussing the financial crisis. Oil prices had skyrocketed, causing severe economic stress. So I began the address with these words: "I'm going to give you ten commandments for surviving the financial crisis."

In seconds, you could hear an onionskin drop on the carpet, so quiet was the audience of 2500 persons. When it was announced that the message would be available on cassette, the telephone operators were kept busy for the next 12 hours trying to handle all the requests.

Everyone is preoccupied. If you know your audience well enough, you will be able to break their preoccupation barrier.

You will rarely find anyone who
wants to know what you think.

You will rarely find anyone who wants to know what you think—not least because so many TV commercials and newspaper ads constantly bombard them with information and invitations. You need to be resourceful to get attention.

Of all the books I've written, one has outsold all the others combined. It has been in print for more than 50 years and translated into 19 languages. The title is *How to Win Over Worry*. Apparently, the title breaks the preoccupation barrier.

You cannot force people to listen to you. If you want them to respond, you must earn the right to be heard. That means you must appeal to their self-interest.

Ineffective leaders ignore this principle. Influential leaders grasp it. Effective leadership occurs only when you break the preoccupation barrier and expose those issues the audience really cares about.

Writers of magazine articles need to break the preoccupation barrier fast, because the reader of the magazine may move on and buy a competing publication instead. One writer who did this effectively used the following first sentence: "You may die before you finish reading this article…"

The sentence is personal. It identifies a potential problem that the reader will want to know about (in this case heart disease). And it applies to everyone. If the first sentence had been, "Heart disease most often strikes men and women around 40…" the writer would immediately have lost a large part of the audience. Only people around 40 would be tempted to read it.

3. Persuade and win by shutting out ego

Many private investors now interact using online bulletin boards. These written conversations record entries by anyone who cares to join in. They allow investors to exchange views and debate issues, and as such they should constitute a hugely valuable resource for anyone invested in a given stock.

But glance over a few bulletin boards and you will soon notice the social incompetence of the contributors. Often they just cannot take opposing views without calling names, making abusive comments, or taking offense. The result: lack of enlightenment and a good deal of wasted energy.

> *Your worst enemy in persuasion is the desire to win arguments.*

Try to remember that your worst enemy in persuasion is the desire to win arguments. You will never gain another person's buy-in through force. If other people don't want to agree with you, they won't. And that spells failure for you.

So pay careful attention to the way you make your case. At every stage, ensure that you do not confuse the legitimate goal of cultivating the other person's support with the illegitimate goal of being seen to be right.

Here are a few strategies you can use to keep out of trouble:

- *Let the other person fully state his position.* Only when he feels you have fully heard and understood him will he show any willingness to hear your reply. So repeat back his objections and let him restate them to you. Get everything out in the open and don't rush to counter point by point.

- *Make it clear you're thinking about it.* Rush in with a rebuttal and he will conclude you haven't been listening. Pause too long and you will appear to have fallen into self-doubt. Get the timing right.

- *Actively seek points of compromise.* There's a reason why the price haggled over by a merchant and his customer always ends up somewhere in the middle. Both sides have to leave the negotiation feeling they have won. Both sides have to leave with their dignity intact. So distinguish between the points you have to win and the ones you can afford to lose. You might say, for example, "That's a very good observation, and I need to reflect on that. But this thought keeps pestering me…"

- *Refer to third parties to resolve clashes of opinion.* Your business partner suggests you redecorate the office in white. You don't feel comfortable with this, but you don't want to have an argument about it. So you suggest doing some Internet research on the effects of office décor on clients. A week later you've discovered a study showing that brilliant white offices remind people of hospitals, and you and your partner buy a few magazines to see what other options are available.

- *Plan the other person's retreat.* Giving up an objection and accepting another person's plan or argument will always pose a threat to the ego. You may have succeeded fully in convincing a colleague that your marketing idea will work better than his, yet he will have difficulty acknowledging this if it means losing face. You can do him, and yourself, a big favor by thinking through in advance how to make this transition easy. Appealing to decisive information helps—"I wouldn't have dreamed of doing it this way if we hadn't looked at that report." So does including the other person in the success—"You know, I started thinking about what you said a few weeks ago…"

4. Persuade and win by speaking efficiently

You may want to ponder these simple rules for improving the persuasiveness of your speaking style:

- *Use layers of proof.* A single statement rarely wins a person over. If I say, "Many people over 60 have gone on to be high achievers," my audience may question the assertion. But I will win their agreement if I then produce repeated proofs. Benjamin Franklin was ambassador to France when more than 80. Gladstone was prime minister of England at 83. Chiang Kai-shek governed the Republic of China when he was more than 80. Verdi wrote operas when he was 80. And so on. You are providing logical and emotional support to convince your listener of what you are saying. Each detail, each fact, builds the argument higher and makes it more compelling.

- *Say it again.* By contrast, restatement offers no additional proof, puts forth no reasons, and gives no details. It simply puts the original thought in fresh language. It says, "Focus your attention on this. Grasp it fully." You should use restatement when you believe greater concentration on the assertion itself is required. Often, a speaker will keep returning to a single statement. This will be the key assertion, the one that he or she wishes the audience to absorb. Explanations can lose an audience. Stories may entertain them, but tend to drift off the point. Coming back to the original assertion focuses the audience's attention on the central issue.

- *Go for big statements.* General illustration amplifies an assertion without giving named examples. This is useful if you don't have named examples at hand. For example, to recommend a school you might say, "Today, this school is turning out some of the nation's best leaders in the fields of robotics, genetic engineering, aerospace, and computer science." The assertion about the quality of the school is backed up without naming any particular individual.

- *Go for small details.* Alternatively—and with greater effect—you can specify names, dates, times, places, incidents. "Professor Smith, the robotics expert at Oxford University, is an alumnus of this school" is more persuasive than a general illustration about the school turning out the "best leaders" in the field.

- *Endorse, endorse, endorse.* Testimony happens when a recognized authority refers to your assertion and says, "I agree." If the audience respects the person giving the testimony, you (or your product or your campaign) will benefit from the endorsement. Just one word of caution: overuse of quotations and testimonies can undermine your audience's confidence in your own power to convince. My former professor, P.B. Fitzwater, said, "People don't come to hear through your lips what somebody else said. They come to hear what you say!"

5. Persuade and win by having an answer to "why?"

Some years ago, a salesman tried to persuade me that I needed a computer in my study at home. I disagreed. I told him, "The cost is prohibitive. I don't have the space. And I have not been trained to use one."

*Usually people don't believe a statement
unless there is concrete proof.*

He didn't let the matter drop. He explained that his company would give me full instructions. He showed me how little space the equipment required. He convinced me that I was losing money by my archaic method of dictating, reviewing, and editing. He demonstrated how failure to secure the equipment was like throwing money in the trash.

I became one of the earliest users and proponents of information technology because that salesman supported his assertion that "You need a computer."

Abstract ideas tend to put people to sleep. Usually people don't believe a statement unless there is concrete proof. And they don't act on a suggestion unless it's given logical and emotional support.

6. Persuade and win by being there

A dear and respected friend of mine has a global television ministry. For years, God has used him to broadcast the message of the Gospel. However, one day he turned up in a city more than 1500 miles (2400 kilometers) from his home.

When asked the purpose of the visit, he said, "I'm here to meet our supporters and to encourage them—and of course to raise funds."

This struck me as odd.

He wanted to touch the world through television, yet when he needed to raise funds he abandoned television and bought an air ticket. He knew that a TV appearance—even if seen by 10,000 people—would not have the same impact as his personal presence.

Impersonal connection has multiplied in the last three decades. We use e-mail, text messaging, websites. Some do their courting on the Internet. But face-to-face communication remains indispensable.

Does not a direct personal encounter trump any courtship in cyberspace? Why do people come in person to the funeral of a dear friend when they could just as well watch a recording of the service?

One of the globe's stellar Christian businessmen, Richard M. (Rich) DeVos, never sends e-mails. If he receives one, he will either pick up the phone or write a letter.

*Whatever you try to persuade others of,
remember that face-to-face communication
holds pride of place.*

Influence in leadership requires that you maximize communication. Don't be fooled by the number of e-mail addresses on your mail server. Contacts do not amount to communication. We have more contacts today, at least in the West, than ever in our history, and less communication. Many people don't even know who lives in the condo next door to them.

I am grateful for every medium by which good leadership and divine truth is communicated. That includes radio, television, iPod, movies, and a host of others. Whatever you try to persuade others of, remember that face-to-face communication holds pride of place.

Summary

Influential leaders always have the ability to persuade effectively.

You can and must acquire this. Make communication an ongoing study, your lifelong passion and discipline. Study human reactions to find out what those around you are thinking. Devise ways to refer to their experience in the achievement of your objectives.

Always distinguish the goal of gaining consent from the goal of beating the opposition. Force and one-upmanship don't achieve persuasion. Your aim is to have others say, "Yes, that's the right way to go," not "Yes, he was right."

Start by listening. People who listen get a reputation for intelligence. Others like them because most people enjoy being listened to. Listening builds confidence and trust. If you do it well, you are more likely to get your point across.

The frequent error of miscommunication can occur in all kinds of ways, but it can be avoided. Don't assume that others will hear what you say the first time and decode the message correctly. If necessary, use "spaced repetition" to ensure that your colleagues absorb the message.

When persuading others to take an action they would not otherwise take, you will need to deal with their preoccupations. In particular, you will have to avoid turning influence into a contest of egos. Remember, if your priority is to gain recognition as the winner, you will neither persuade nor win. Influential leaders don't have to browbeat their opponents or be right on every detail. The measure of their influence is the degree to which others voluntarily follow their lead.

STEP 7

DECIDE TO INVEST FEARLESSLY

In 1981, I returned to the lovely island of Bali in Indonesia. Since rooms were tight, I did not stay at my usual stopping place, the Bali Intercontinental, but instead secured accommodations at the Bali Hyatt.

When I arrived and started up the steps to the entrance, the head bellman said, "Welcome to the Bali Hyatt, Dr. Haggai. We've reserved the Presidential Suite for you."

I protested that I had reserved a minimum rate single room.

"The general manager insists," he said. "He wants you to charge everything to the room—your laundry, dry cleaning, meals, telephone—everything. You are his guest."

At the registration desk an assistant swept me through.

"Oh, no, that is already taken care of," he said. "Let me escort you to your suite."

It was one of the most elegant accommodations I had seen in all of my world travels. Within minutes, the general manager, Michael Ou, arrived to greet me. Stunned, I tried to express my thanks.

"You don't remember me, do you?" he said.

I had to confess I didn't.

> *"I have harbored a secret dream for all these years*
> *that someday I would run my own*
> *hotel and be able to show you gratitude*
> *for the inspiration you gave me."*

"In the 1960s when you stayed at the Singapore Intercontinental, I was a bellman, hustling bags. Every time you came, you treated me just as grandly as you treated your friend, the general manager, George Milne. I have harbored a secret dream for all these years that someday I would run my own hotel and be able to show you gratitude for the encouragement and inspiration you gave me."

Not long afterward, at Brisbane Airport, Australia, I found myself stranded when my plane to Sydney was grounded for maintenance. Never have I heard airport personnel so verbally abused. The frustrated passengers erupted toward the attendants. Finally, the manager came out, and the cursing and invectives hit a new crescendo.

When everyone had left, I walked to the manager's office and asked for a brief word. I think he was expecting a complaint.

I said, "I deal with world leaders on every continent, and I applaud the way you handled this riotous situation. You're headed for the stars. I just wanted you to know. Success to you."

His response would have suggested lockjaw. I shook his hand and left.

A year later, I was at the same counter to catch an Ansett Airways plane to another city. The desk clerk said, "Dr. Haggai, you have Seat 2B in first class."

As was my custom, I had reserved an economy seat. When I pointed this out, however, the desk clerk told me the manager had left instructions that whenever Dr. John Edmund Haggai showed up for a flight, he should be upgraded to first class.

I have never practiced courtesy in the hope of cashing in on someone else's gratitude. It's just a visionary decision to invest in relationships. It costs me nothing. It honors the Lord. It's obedience to His commands. It just happens to pay big dividends!

As a friend told me years ago, "Cast thy bread upon the waters, and after many days it will come back—toasted."

More than once, a world leader has said, "I believe you know more people than anyone." Another opined, "Every place Haggai stops overseas, they treat him like a head of state."

If that's so, I neither ask for it nor regard it as owed to me. It's because my relationships stem from more than a handshake in a reception line or a photo-op at a dinner. I consciously give in every situation I'm in.

Fearless Investment Pays

When *Forbes* magazine interviewed the Chinese industrialist Robert Kuok, they made the following observation:

> Kuok may not be the biggest player in Asia. We estimate his family's net worth to be at least $7 billion. But for sheer versatility, imagination and ability to get things done, he has no peer.
>
> "What could take us 18 to 24 months [in China], Kuok's Kerry Group could do in 2 months," says John Farrell, president of Coca-Cola China Ltd. "His whole life has been built around building networks with overseas Chinese and in China. The Kerry Group's ability to do things fast is incredible."
>
> "I adapt like a chameleon to the particular society where I am operating at the moment," Kuok says. Robert Riley, managing director of Mandarin Oriental Hotel Group, a fierce Kuok competitor, says: "He's a local everywhere he goes."[20]

Like many in Asia, Kuok invests in relationships. But he is "a local everywhere he goes" not only because he is Chinese, but because "his whole life has been built around building networks"—and *guanxi*. He gets help from people in his circle because he has gone to the trouble of cultivating those relationships.

Kuok illustrates the benefits of investing, in the widest sense of the term. He understands that when you give something, you will receive it back many times over. Some in the West have called this the Law of Reciprocity or The Golden Rule. But as much as people pay lip service to the principle, few seem to live by it.

> *What do you want? Invest the same thing,*
> *and you will receive it back in quantity.*

The Bible tells us, "Whatever a man sows, that he will also reap." It's just a fact. What do you want? Invest the same thing, and you will receive it back in quantity. Do you want friends? Invest friendship. Do you want love? Invest love. Do you want respect? Invest by respecting others.

You receive back what you invest. How much you receive back depends on how much you invest. If you invest little, you will receive little in return; but if you invest a lot, you will receive a lot. Robert Kuok receives back—in multiples—the business friendship he spends much time cultivating. And that means profit for him.

Fearless Investment Equals Giving

I use the terms *investment* and *giving* interchangeably. In other words, I invest in numerous ways (time, relationships, learning, charitable donations) with exactly the same optimistic expectation of return as I have when I make a financial investment.

To many people, *giving* implies a reduction in the giver's net worth. If they give away $100, they think they will be $100 dollars poorer as a result. Consequently they are afraid to give. They clutch everything close for fear of losing it.

But this is a scarcity mentality. It equates giving with losing. In reality, the reverse applies. The term *investment* carries the idea of increasing the investor's net worth. Those who understand this have an abundance mentality. They realize that the more they give away—in time, money, or encouragement—the more they will receive back.

An influential leader invests habitually. He does not do this because he *expects* a reward, but because he *knows* that rewards flow from this kind of behavior. When Michael Ou was a bellhop at the Intercontinental, I had no idea I would ever meet him again. Still less did I calculate that he might do me a handsome favor 20 years down the road. I just knew that politeness made life more enjoyable for everyone, and that this was a win-win outcome at almost no cost to me.

I am not a saint. Nobody is. In reality, self-interest motivates all our giving and investment—and there's nothing wrong with that. People who give significant money to charities do so because they want recognition, or because they feel pity or peer pressure or guilt, or because it pleases them to do good. No stigma attaches to it. Those who invest by donating money derive legitimate gain and satisfaction. Frankly, were that not so, nobody would ever give. It's just human nature.

Investment represents a visionary decision to give freely, as often as you can, within the bounds of sound discipline and good sense.

The point is, you don't need to fear investment of any kind. Investment represents a visionary decision to give freely, as often as you can, within the bounds of sound discipline and good sense. Remember also that you set the tone as a leader. If your leadership is characterized by love, humility, and self-discipline, you will reap loyalty and devotion from the people you lead. If they recognize that you invest your very life for their good, they will more readily follow your leadership and example.

In a previous chapter, I mentioned Dr. Han. The elders of Dr. Han's church in Korea once gave me a striking insight into his generosity. They paid him his salary every Friday. But often, before he arrived home, he had given it all away. Finally, they started giving the money to Mrs. Han so she could pay the bills and buy the groceries! Dr. Han's practice of giving accorded his leadership the credibility and permanence that self-serving leaders never attain. It also had a lasting impact on those he led.

> *When you take the visionary decision to*
> *give fearlessly, and when you receive back*
> *what you give out, others will notice.*

When you understand investment and practice it yourself, you instill it in the members of your group. When you take the visionary decision to give fearlessly, and when you receive back what you give out, others will notice.

I have read few analyses of business success that outpace the classic *In Search of Excellence* by Thomas J. Peters and Robert H. Waterman Jr. Among eight qualities highlighted, they note: "Excellent companies are close to the customer." Such companies have an obsession with standards, reliability, and service. They are committed to making the customer important, giving him the best value for his money, and being ready to serve him in any way he needs. Such excellent companies reap what they sow by gaining customer loyalty and long-term sales and profit growth.

Peters and Waterman tell the story of Frito-Lay, an American snack food company, to illustrate the point:

> What is striking about Frito is not its brand-management system, which is solid, nor its advertising program, which is well done. What is striking is Frito's nearly 10,000-person

sales force and its "99.9% service level." In practical terms, what does this mean? It means that Frito will do some things that in the short run clearly are uneconomic. It will spend several hundred dollars sending a truck to restock a store with a couple of $30 cartons of potato chips. You don't make money that way, it would seem. But the institution is filled with tales of salesmen braving extraordinary weather to deliver a box of potato chips or to help a store clean up after a hurricane or an accident. Letters about such acts pour into the Dallas headquarters. There are magic and symbolism about the service call that cannot be quantified. As we said earlier, it is a cost analyst's dream target. You can always make a case for saving money by cutting back a percentage point or two. But Frito management, looking at market shares and margins, won't tamper with the zeal of the sales force.[21]

As a result of this sowing of service, Frito-Lay reaps more than two billion dollars of potato chip and pretzel sales per year. It owns market shares of 60 percent and 70 percent in most of America (astoundingly high for such an undifferentiated product), and has profit margins that are the envy of the food industry.

Influential leaders make investment habitual. Two kinds of people make up the world: the investors and the takers. Investors see the "potent" in potential and capitalize on it. By contrast, the takers do not see giving as an investment and try to hoard whatever they have. Ultimately, the investors win and the takers lose.

$188 Million in a Year

If you've traveled the world as a student, you probably have stayed in a YMCA hostel.

A long-serving leader of the YMCA, John R. Mott, who was born in 1865 and died in his ninetieth year, is one of the world's great unsung heroes. Besides his YMCA involvement, Mott set up the International

Missionary Council. He headed up a fund-raising drive for the United War Work Council that raised more than $188 million in less than a year. He recruited more than 240,000 men and women for leadership positions on all six continents during the course of his unequaled career. He was decorated by 18 nations. He won the Nobel Peace Prize in 1946. You cannot worship at any church of any denomination on any continent that he did not influence.

The key to John Mott's leadership was fearless giving. John Mott represents the highest type of leadership. No personality cult arose around his name. Mott was generous with his concepts, his time, his energy, and his money.

> *America's position as a world superpower can be attributed, in large measure, to its generosity.*

I believe that America's position as a world superpower can be attributed, in large measure, to its generosity. Over the years, America has given more money, goods, and services to other nations than all the rest of the world combined. I believe America's global leadership role correlates closely with this investment of concern and resources.

Yet we see Asians increasingly taking up John Mott's mantle.

Wendy Yap, a trustee of Haggai Institute International, recently testified about her motives for releasing money for the new training center. She had been studying in the Gospels about the Lord's feeding of the five thousand. "When they asked the Lord what the people were going to do since they had not eaten, He asked them what they had."

Wendy pointed out that the Lord didn't swing into action until they gave Him what resources they already possessed—in this case, five loaves and two fish.

Then she said, "As I thought about that, I realized that we had committed two million dollars; that would be like two fish. Now I think we must provide the loaves."

For nearly 40 years, I have watched men and women in leadership roles. The takers ultimately lose. They lose money, friends, health, and respect. The investors win. As a leader, you need to master the meaning of investment and study how to make giving a habit—for both you and those you lead.

Why Ineffective Leaders Don't Invest

Logic compels us to build fearless investment into our visionary decision making. Investment has built into it the motive of legitimate individual self-interest. Everyone wins.

The idea underlies all economics and ultimately all expenditure of effort. We exert ourselves—give out our energy—to achieve a result. The farmer gains by giving. He invests his labor and seed and irrigation into the soil. He normally gets back in proportion to what he puts in. The businessman gains by widening the market. He invests money for advertising and entertainment and public relations and necessary travel and labor. He gets his money back multiplied. The athlete invests effort and gains strength and achievement in proportion to the effort invested.

> *The influential leader will appeal to the powerful desire of self-interest to encourage his people to invest.*

The influential leader, therefore, will appeal to the powerful desire of self-interest to encourage his people to invest. Some will object that giving for selfish motives does not qualify as giving. But this is nonsense. The returns on fearless giving are as inexorable as the law of gravitation. The leader brings benefit to everyone, including himself, when he successfully motivates others to invest through self-interest.

Only three things deter people from taking this step.

Risk-aversion

Unwillingness to take risks often results in refusal to give. But no more risk attaches to generosity than to any other kind of business investment. Giving fearlessly demands that you make yourself vulnerable.

Without risk, there is no forward movement.

When the farmer puts the seed into the ground, he becomes vulnerable to the risk of bad weather. He will not see the seed again for a period of time, during which he will cultivate, water, and employ all of the agricultural techniques he knows to insure an abundant harvest. When a businessman invests in a piece of property, he becomes vulnerable. Without vulnerability, there is no viability. Without risk, there is no forward movement.

Miserliness

Second, people refuse to give because they are greedy. This desire to possess things often disguises itself as something more respectable. People camouflage stinginess with such expressions as "prudence" or "good business" or "sound planning." But being miserly comes down to an obsession with possessions. You refuse to give what you own, and you desire for yourself the property of others.

A miserly mindset can give you ulcers, shatter your friendships, and subject you to unnecessary stress. The costs in litigations, medical care, and forced vacations can easily offset the short-term gain of miserly maneuvers.

Insecurity

Insecure people don't give. Instead they feel compelled to direct all their efforts to self-defense. Transfixed by fear, the insecure person does his best to protect himself from calamity. No matter how much bravado he projects, in reality fear rules his every thought. And, of course, a temperament governed by insecurity and fear does not make for great leadership.

Visionary Decisions to Help You Invest Fearlessly

Dwight L. Moody was not timid when it came to asking for money. Time after time, he had solicited funds from the businessman James Farwell. On one occasion, after Moody had asked Farwell for $10,000, Farwell complained, "Mr. Moody, must you always be coming to me for money? You have so many other wealthy friends. I've already given you $85,000 for your work."

Moody replied, "Mr. Farwell, you grew up on a farm, just as I did. Did you ever take a pail to a dry cow?"

Moody's leadership developed Farwell, but Moody's influence with Farwell would have died had Farwell not known that Moody was a self-giving person who practiced what he preached. Largely through Moody's influence, Farwell became an outstanding nineteenth-century philanthropist.

The only motive Jesus ever appealed to was the motive of self-interest. He represented investment through self-interest as the path to permanent gain. Every command He gave and every promise He made assumed self-interest on the part of the hearer.

For example, Jesus said, "Judge not, that you be not judged" (Matthew 7:1). He also said, "Do not lay up for yourselves treasures on earth, where moth and rust destroy and where thieves break in and steal; but lay up for yourselves treasures in heaven" (Matthew 6:19).

The leader's attitude toward money and material possessions will impact the effectiveness of his leadership. If you want to get giving right, resolve to make these visionary decisions.

1. Invest fearlessly by keeping your mind on the things you want

Fear the worst, and usually you'll get it.

Our negative thoughts and fears become self-fulfilling prophecies. If you don't believe you will make your sales goal, you probably won't. If you are a manager, and you are afraid your new team won't accept you, they probably won't. If you tell a child that he will fail and never amount to any good, you'll probably be right.

There's a difference between seeing a glass as half-empty and seeing it as half-full. The water level doesn't change. The difference lies in your attitude. You will ruin your leadership potential if you concentrate on the things you don't want.

The leader who gives fearlessly tends to become positive and optimistic. This increases his personal power and influence.

Experience shows that if you keep your mind on the things you want, you'll probably succeed. Keep your mind on winning the race and you boost your chances of coming in first. Tell a friend he can accomplish a difficult task and you boost the chances of him succeeding.

The leader who gives fearlessly tends to become positive and optimistic. This increases his personal power and influence.

2. Invest fearlessly by considering what you want to get back

This seems like an obvious statement. If you plant cotton, what do you get? Cotton. If you plant wheat, what do you get? Wheat. If you plant corn, what do you get? Corn. If you plant friendship, what do you get? Friends.

Most people will agree with me that far. The awkward part comes when you ask, "If you invest money, what do you get?" Many people are reluctant to admit that, in a general sense, giving away money causes money to come back. Yet, in my experience, that is exactly what happens. So if you are short of cash, don't hoard the little you've got. Give some away. From a financial standpoint, it's the best thing you can do.

3. Invest fearlessly by emphasizing initiative

Suppose a farmer were to say, "If I have a good harvest, I'll then plant the seed." Or suppose a businessman were to say, "When I receive 100 percent of the lease payments for a ten-year period, I'll build the apartment building." Both are ridiculous!

If you are short of cash, don't hoard the little you've got. Give some away. From a financial standpoint, it's the best thing you can do.

No, you invest *first*—on the front end. Don't delude yourself by saying, "When my ship comes in I will give a lot of money to help people in need." Start where you are, with what you have.

In the early 1980s, downtown Holland, Michigan, resembled every other downtown of the period. It faced rising competition from malls and larger superstores, made worse because heavy winter snowfalls made it an unfriendly environment for shoppers.

Then local businessman and property developer Ed Prince had a brilliant idea. Why not, he thought, place a network of tough plastic tubing under the sidewalks, and then circulate warm water using waste heat from the power plant?

As often happens with new ideas, initially the proposal got a thumbs-down. The Holland Board of Public Works, operator of the power plant, opposed the initiative in spite of Ed's offer of a major financial contribution. In the end, the project squeaked past the city council by a single vote.

Today, former critics of the Streetscape Project and its downtown snowmelt system acknowledge it as a key factor in the area's revival. The Board of Public Works has even featured the snowmelt system on the cover of its annual report. A colleague made the following comment:

> Prince was a visionary, but he was an excellent judge of people to get involved in the project. His ability to help others see how the pieces of the puzzle fit together got people excited about their part in the collaborative effort. He then stepped back from the project and let others have the limelight. It appears that he received satisfaction from being involved in the project. He did not seek or want earthly praise; at many times he even rejected the gestures.

4. Invest fearlessly by practicing patience

When the farmer plants, he doesn't expect a crop the next day. It takes months. It may be a while. You may have lots of other matters to attend to before the harvest. Farmers don't sit at the edge of the field with binoculars, or dig the seeds up to make sure they are germinating. Relax. Keep cool. Patience is the mark of the influential leader.

5. Invest fearlessly by tolerating disappointment

I live in Atlanta, Georgia. Just because a frost ruins the peach crop in Georgia, does the peach farmer quit growing peaches? No, he knows that he will prosper as he obeys the laws of peach growing.

Just because a friend betrays you, does that mean you should never trust anyone else? I hope not. You may say, "I invested love, and I was betrayed. I invested friendship, and I was insulted. I invested money, and I suffered financial disaster." True, life gives no guarantees. But the law of planting and harvesting works. Over the long term you will prosper.

6. Invest fearlessly by staying cheerful

Even when things are not going right, stay cheerful. You can't think clearly when you're frowning and fretting.

Think and act the way you ought to feel. Soon you will feel the way you are thinking and acting.

You may not feel on top of the world if you have just lost some money in a sour investment or the stock market just dived by 40 percent. While you can't control your feelings directly, you can control them indirectly by controlling your actions and thoughts. Think and act the way you ought to feel. Soon you will feel the way you are thinking and acting.

Nobody follows a person who complains. There are two types of people: thermometers and thermostats. The thermometer person, who registers the temperature of his environment, goes up and down like a yo-yo. He reacts according to whatever happens to him.

The thermostat person regulates the temperature of his environment. When this radiant personality comes in the room, you feel like a hundred lights have switched on. Resolve to have that effect on others. Let others see your positive attitude.

7. Invest fearlessly by expecting results

The farmer expects results. He may not see any evidence for several weeks, but he expects results. The influential leader should expect results too. He should expect that when he invests encouragement in a person, he will see better performance. He should expect that when he goes out of his way to show friendship, he will acquire many friends. And he should expect that when he invests money, he will get money back.

This habit will add an impressive dimension to your leadership. You'll always seem in command—focused, energized, in control of yourself. That inspires confidence and loyalty.

8. Invest fearlessly by being thankful

When your investment pays off, you will feel a strong urge to congratulate yourself. You worked hard, you planned well, you sacrificed.

But don't be fooled. The returns on giving are written into the way the universe works. So let your life and leadership exemplify fearless giving, and leave a mark of beneficial permanence. I challenge you, if you have not made this visionary decision before, to do so today.

Summary

If you invest fearlessly by giving, you will receive it back in larger quantities. What you receive back will depend on what you invested (for example, if you invest friendship, you will have many friends) and on how much you invested.

There is nothing wrong with giving out of self-interest. The investor invests because it will benefit him. As a leader, you need to acknowledge and practice this principle. In addition, you should instill into the people in your group the habit of giving.

There are two kinds of people in the world: investors and takers. The investors practice the principle of investment by nature. The takers are the ones who do not see giving as an investment and try to hoard whatever they have. Ultimately, the investors win because they receive back many times what they invested. The takers ultimately lose because they lose money, friends, health, and respect.

To master fearless giving, you should bear in mind a number of guidelines. Invest what you want to get back. Keep your mind on the outcomes you want, not on those you are trying to avoid. Invest on the front end, not when you are already financially secure. Practice patience, especially when things go wrong in the short-term. Maintain a cheerful state of mind. Also, expect results—and be thankful whether you get them immediately or not.

DECIDE TO PROFIT FROM THE IMPOSSIBLE

Opportunity and impossibility represent two sides of the same coin.

World stock markets crash. Billions of dollars are wiped off the value of blue chip multinationals. Investors rush for the exits, settling for anything rather than nothing. The colossal re-rating bumps downward until the price of stocks reflects the meager amounts investors are now willing to pay. Most lose out heavily. Many face ruin.

There is no better time to buy.

In every wall of impossibility you'll find
a small gate called opportunity.

In every wall of impossibility you'll find a small gate called opportunity. The more impossible the situation, the greater the opportunity it contains. If you want to succeed, seek out an impossible situation—a place where things seem to have reached a no-way-out conclusion, in finance, in scholarship, in relationships. Even—perhaps especially—if the impossibility flows from your own mistakes.

Dr. Peter Okaalet serves as senior director for Health and HIV/AIDS

Policy at MAP (Medical Assistance Programs) International. In 1987, he attended Haggai Institute and as a result, a seed was sown that would germinate just a year later when a close family friend died of AIDS.

His friend's death marked a crisis both personal and professional. Personally, he was bereaved. As a doctor, it was almost more than he could bear to hold a dying man in his arms and say, "I have no more solutions to offer you."

His own failure was compounded by that of the clergy. Time and again, Peter would see ministers greet their AIDS patients not from the bedside but nervously from the door of the ward. Ignorance and terror rendered them unable to function.

An incurable disease rampaging the country. A church too terrified to help. It seemed an impossible situation.

But that was the moment Peter Okaalet caught a vision. He himself would bridge the gap between medicine and ministry and engage the Christian church in the fight against HIV and AIDS in Africa.

He attended Nairobi Evangelical Graduate School of Theology to earn a Masters in Divinity and Theology. Then he began a campaign to establish education about HIV/AIDS as a permanent feature of the theological curriculum.

At the time of this writing, 1349 students in 14 institutions are receiving this instruction. Already, 230 have graduated with HIV/AIDS counseling certificates from colleges and institutions across six African countries—Kenya, South Africa, Tanzania, Uganda, Zambia, and Zimbabwe. In 2005, *Time* magazine recognized his work and named him one of its "Global Health Heroes."

Peter Okaalet knows how to profit from the impossible.

Impossibility in Business

Seeing business opportunities is a skill for which Americans have long been renowned. But it's amazing how many times opportunities crop up just at the moment you feel like giving up.

Take Levi Strauss jeans. Nobody would wear jeans today had it not been for Levi Strauss's business partner Jacob Davis.

Originally a dry goods merchant, Levi Strauss had arrived in San Francisco at the age of 24. Since then he had earned a reputation both as a businessman and as a philanthropist. Davis had been one of his customers—a tailor working out of Reno, Nevada, who came to San Francisco to buy bolts of cloth.

One day, a client came to Davis's store and showed him the pants he'd bought the previous week. The pockets were torn off. Davis repaired them. The next week the man came back with the same problem—as did other clients too. For manual laborers, the pockets on normal pants just weren't up to carrying tools. Increasing amounts of Davis's time got swallowed up fixing his own product.

It was a problem—and also an opportunity.

Suddenly, Davis hit on the idea of placing metal rivets at the points of strain—at the pocket corners and the base of the button fly. These riveted trousers were an instant success with everyone, so much so that Davis began to worry that someone might steal his great idea. So he decided to take out a patent on the process, but he couldn't afford the $68 required to file the papers.

So he wrote to Levi Strauss to suggest that the two of them hold the patent together. Astute enough to see the potential for the new product, Strauss agreed to Davis's proposal. They received patent #139,121 from the U.S. Patent and Trademark Office on 20 May 1873. The rest is history.

Or look at the life of automobile mogul Lee Iacocca.

In the 1970s, Lee Iacocca was the aggressive, successful president of the Ford Motor Company. He had created the Mustang, a car that sold more units its first year than any other automobile in history. He had led Ford to a $1.8 billion profit for two years in a row.

He received an income of $970,000 a year and was treated royally. But he lived in the shadow of Henry Ford II, a man Iacocca described as capricious and spiteful. On 13 July 1978, Henry Ford fired Lee Iacocca.

Less than four months later, Iacocca became president of Chrysler, an automobile company that had just announced a third-quarter loss of $160 million, the worst deficit it had ever suffered. Iacocca found that Chrysler was poorly managed. Each of the 31 vice presidents was working by himself rather than working as part of the team.

The oil shortage of 1979 compounded Chrysler's problems as the price of gasoline almost doubled and sales of large cars plummeted. In 1980, Chrysler lost $1.7 billion, until then the largest operating loss in United States corporate history.

But Iacocca was turning his impossibilities into opportunities. He had been fired. He had become president of a company most people felt would go bankrupt. But without these obstacles, Lee Iacocca would never have had a chance to prove himself. He was determined not to quit. He won concessions from the unions. He streamlined Chrysler's operation and developed new products.

In 1982, Chrysler made a modest profit. In 1983, it made the best profit in its history, enabling the company to pay off its controversial government-guaranteed loan seven years before it was due.

Under Iacocca's leadership, Chrysler introduced new cars that excited the American public: the economical K-car, convertibles, and the minivan. Chrysler stock soared from two dollars to thirty-six dollars a share. Its investors made money and gained renewed confidence in the company. Its challenging slogan became known nationwide: "If you can find a better built car, buy it!"

Lee Iacocca became one of the most respected corporate leaders in America, and when his autobiography was published in 1984, it broke publishing sales records.

When It All Goes Wrong

But what if you've been the author of your own downfall? What if the impossible situation arises, wholly or partly, from your own short-sightedness or incompetence? Can you still profit from it?

The answer is yes.

As a young man, Moses made the mistake of intervening in a fight and killing an Egyptian slave driver. No doubt his motives were good. Nevertheless, when news leaked out, he was in trouble. Far from championing the cause of the Israelites at the Egyptian court, he now had to flee for his life. He spent the next few decades in exile.

As he looked after his father-in-law's sheep in the desert, no doubt Moses reflected ruefully on that mistake—one he looked unlikely to recover from. How could a man guilty of murder regain credibility among his own people, let alone escape capture and death at the hands of the Egyptian authorities? It was impossible.

---

*Since you are bound to make blunders, you must
know how to turn blunders into benefits.*

But Moses did come back. And so can you.

The first thing to do is recognize your weakness. You are not perfect. Nor am I. Nor is anyone. Since you are bound to make blunders—a mistake made through stupidity, ignorance, or carelessness—you must know how to turn blunders into benefits.

Anyone can succeed in ideal conditions. That kind of success takes no genius. You demonstrate genius when your success grows out of failure. You prove your character if you can refrain from throwing up your hands in despair.

Visionary Decisions to Help You Profit from the Impossible

Influential leaders make mistakes. But they have taken visionary decisions that help them sidestep paralysis and self-doubt and learn from their mistakes and capitalize on them. Resolve to take these visionary decisions to help you profit from the impossible.

1. Profit from the impossible by admitting mistakes fast

You can never correct a problem if you don't admit that it exists. Moreover, mistakes multiply and get worse if they are left uncorrected.

When NASA, the American space agency, first sent a probe to Venus, scientists were careful to monitor its progress. If the probe had veered just one degree off course, it would have missed its target by approximately 200,000 miles.

> *You can never correct a problem*
> *if you don't admit that it exists.*

Late in 1969, I learned that Haggai Institute's accountant had forgotten my instructions to pay an airline bill of nearly $50,000 for bringing the participants and faculty to the organization's first training session. The accountant had used the money to pay some smaller, less pressing bills, leaving no funds for the airline.

Like the proverbial ostrich, I stuck my head in the sand, hoping the problem would go away. I didn't want to admit the blunder had been made. As a result, we lost our international airline credit cards.

The airline threatened us repeatedly with lawsuits. It wasn't until I admitted the error, talked to the creditors, and transparently told them what we could do and what we could not do that the fears began to subside, the doubt melted, and the limitations seemed to disappear.

2. Profit from the impossible by taking responsibility

No one likes to assume responsibility for mistakes. Observe the behavior of your colleagues over the next few days and note how they will distance themselves from things that go wrong.

This started in the Garden of Eden. When God caught up with Adam and Eve after they had eaten the fruit of the tree of the knowledge of good and evil, He asked Adam if he had eaten it. Adam's response was exactly what we see today: he denied responsibility and passed the buck. "The woman whom You gave to be with me, she gave me of the tree, and I ate." Eve did the same thing. "The serpent deceived me, and I ate" (Genesis 3:12-13).

> *The people with the greatest number*
> *of achievements have frequently*
> *messed up the most often.*

Mistakes happen all the time. No one escapes them. In fact, the people with the greatest number of achievements have frequently messed up the most often. As commentators love to point out, Babe Ruth's record number of home runs in one season went hand in hand with a record number of strikeouts.

To correct and profit from your mistakes you must assume responsibility for them. As a leader, you must also assume responsibility for the mistakes of the people in your group—just as you receive credit and respect for the group's successes. Influential leaders do not pass blame down the management line. When they have to, they take the hit.

Mistakes are a beginning, not an end, as long as you keep yourself accountable.

3. Profit from the impossible by bravely evaluating the damage

Will the damage resulting from this mistake be great or small? Think it through carefully. Do not underestimate nor overestimate it.

Sometimes we can get embarrassed because a mistake causes us to lose face while actually sustaining little real damage. At other times, that very embarrassment makes us want to cover up by downplaying the consequences. That way lies danger. If real damage has occurred, a leader should take quick and drastic measures to prevent further loss.

When we launched Haggai Institute for Advanced Leadership Training, we took great care to choose a neutral location. If we had placed our training center in the United States, outsiders might have accused our alumni of being Uncle Toms or mouthpieces for America's CIA. A host of leaders from Asia, Africa, South America, and Australia affirmed Switzerland as the ideal nation.

---

*Conducting the initial seminars of
Haggai Institute in Switzerland turned into
one of the biggest mistakes we ever made.*

Yet conducting the initial seminars of Haggai Institute in Switzerland turned into one of the biggest mistakes we ever made. Switzerland was not the right place. When the owner of a property went back on his commitment to sell, we incurred a cash loss of $55,000.

I had no choice but to admit the mistake. I called a major donor who had borrowed $100,000 to get the program started and made an appointment to see him. I would rather have taken a flogging, but I knew I had to do it.

"Why can't you tell me by phone what's on your mind?" he asked.

"Regarding this matter," I said, "I must sit in front of you and look into your eyes."

This dear man could have made life miserable for me. But when I arrived at his home and told him the story, he broke out in a big grin and said, "John, you learned a great lesson by a much cheaper mistake than I did. We have just lost two million dollars on a bad overseas venture in our business!"

What grace!

It became clear that I had been influenced to move to Switzerland by superficial reasons—the offer of property in a beautiful area at a low price. I had fallen prey to the trap of taking what was handy and attractive rather than what was really needed.

Changing course wasn't easy. We lost momentum and incurred further costs finding a new location in another part of the world.

When evaluating the damage done by a mistake, ask yourself such questions as: What effects will it have on project deadlines? How will this mistake interfere with the work of others? Will it adversely affect the big picture—the long-term goals of the organization?

4. Profit from the impossible by studying the causes of the failure

> *Failing to understand the causes of your mistake will only guarantee a repetition.*

Examine all the possible explanations in depth. Failing to understand the causes of your mistake will only guarantee a repetition. Cross-examine yourself. Remember, pushing blame away to others amounts to leadership suicide. Identify the problem in yourself and isolate it. For example:

- *Was the planning defective?* You may have planned most of the project, but if you overlooked any component, the whole project could suffer.

- *Did you choose the right time?* I once met an American who had taken 30 people to stage an outdoor event in an Asian country. He had not reckoned on the monsoons, and because of his poor timing, hundreds of thousands of dollars were wasted.

- *Was the project sufficiently funded?* Business people frequently make the mistake of setting out with insufficient funds, believing that money will somehow turn up at a later stage. It seldom does. So be tough-minded about future costs and don't forget to allow for inflation.

- *Did you have adequate personnel?* Did you have the various jobs slotted, and did you know exactly the person or persons required to fill each slot? Did you have a sufficient number of people both in the skilled and the nonskilled areas?

- *Did you have the right kind of equipment?* For example, if you needed to send out large mailings, did you have the means to process them? Or did the lack of equipment mean that the mailing was stretched over a long period, thus neutralizing the impact?

- *Did you anticipate and make contingency plans for possible obstructions?* For instance, in certain countries one must make provision for strikes. Did you allow for sickness or legitimate absenteeism? Did you make plans for securing any necessary government clearances or permissions?

- *Was your information accurate?* Someone once said to me: "A genius with poor information will always come in second to a mediocre man with good information." He was so right.

- *Did you brief people correctly?* Ask yourself if the mistake resulted from staff failing to understand your instructions. You're not looking for scapegoats, but trying to perfect your lines of communication.

5. Profit from the impossible by immediately eliminating the causes

Your evaluation should reveal the causes of the error. Now take action. Write down your plan. Work this into your goals program.

Conducting the Haggai Institute seminars in Switzerland was a mistake for several reasons:

- The late 1960s was a time of hijacking sprees. Developing world leaders from the Orient did not like the prospect of refueling in Middle Eastern capitals plagued by terrorists.

- The climate and cuisine of Switzerland were unsuitable for most leaders from other nations.

- Although the leaders coming for the international training all spoke English, few of them spoke German. If any difficulties with airline connections arose, the leaders would have difficulty contacting us. Most didn't know enough German to even ask for an English-speaking telephone operator.

- The facility we were using was two-and-a-half hours from the nearest airport in Zurich. Picking people up and returning them became a logistical nightmare.

- When most people think of Switzerland, they think of numbered bank accounts, expensive ski holidays, and high-priced vacations. They don't think of human suffering and need. That made fundraising for a ministry based in Switzerland difficult.

Out of this error came a painful conclusion and a complicated transition: a move to Singapore.

Singapore, just as neutral as Switzerland, lies in the heart of the developing world. The climate and cuisine of Singapore are more acceptable to the majority of people attending our seminars. Singapore has a good racial mix, with 85 percent speaking English. The entire Republic of Singapore covers only 230 square miles, facilitating navigation. Not least, Singapore is without question the cleanest major city in the world. Its very orderliness, predictability, and good government are all models for observation by leaders coming from other nations.

6. Profit from the impossible by salvaging what you can

Years ago, a company overproduced hundreds of thousands of fly swatters. It could not handle the expensive inventory and storage requirements, and so it engaged one of the world's leading persuaders, Elmer Wheeler.

Wheeler looked at the fly swatters, noticed that they were square, and suggested the sales line, "These fly swatters are square so you can kill flies in the corners." In a matter of a few weeks, all the fly swatters were sold. This company used good judgment. To secure the services of Elmer Wheeler cost a fortune, but it was a wise expenditure based on a calculated risk. The situation was salvaged.

7. Profit from the impossible by revising your method to avoid a repetition

You should constantly evaluate what you do to see if you can improve upon it—not just in relation to this one mistake but also in relation to all your activities. This requires constant questioning and study.

*Learn from others. Devour biographies.
Read journals related to your field.*

Learn from others. Devour biographies. Read journals related to your field. My heart becomes heavy when I talk to aspiring leaders who have not read even five books in the last year, and who have done nothing to enlarge their knowledge or sharpen their skills.

Continually learn from the experience of others so that you won't reinvent the wheel. When you read biographies and talk to other leaders, write down what you learn and apply those lessons to your own situation.

My own knowledge of leadership and other subjects has come from many sources. I am indebted to teachers and examples from every country and every age, including John Sung of China, Han Kyung Chik of Korea, Benjamin Moraes of Brazil, John Calvin of Geneva, Roland Payne of Liberia, John Wesley of England, Sam Arai of Japan, Baki Sadaka of Egypt, Martin Luther of Germany, Neson Cornelius of India, and Saint Francis Xavier of Spain. My reading covers journals as diverse as *Korean Review, Asia Week, Boardroom Report, Success,* and *Forbes.*

But action must follow learning. Put your revision into practice. In the Haggai Institute program, we used to make the error of scheduling sessions too close to the Chinese New Year. This caused great problems in logistics, image, and faculty availability. We admitted the mistake, assumed responsibility, evaluated the damage, studied the cause, salvaged the situation, and revised the calendar. Today we do no scheduling near the Chinese New Year.

8. Profit from the impossible by beginning to execute the new program immediately

In 1970, James Howard was the 42-year-old head of the sixth largest public relations agency in America. But he felt out of control. He was unhappy with the way he saw some of his clients doing business, and this led to a nervous breakdown. He sold the agency, moved to the quiet state of Vermont, and began to put himself and his career back together.

It would seem as if James Howard had failed. But out of the impossible obstacle of his nervous breakdown came Howard's greatest opportunity. He took the time to discover himself. He wrote out his vision and mission and a new set of goals. He analyzed four sample brokerage businesses he might want to pursue: farm and timber, solar homes, real estate, and small businesses. From this emerged Country Business Services, America's most successful small business brokerage firm. James Howard carefully and systematically turned his obstacle into an opportunity.

When your project goes wrong, procrastination will only make the situation worse. Begin your correction right away. As you embark on the new course, maintain a detailed chart of progress so that you will know exactly where you are at every stage of the program.

The high productivity of post-war Japanese business owes much to W. Edwards Deming and his ideas on Total Quality Management. One of Deming's suggestions was that managers should know—by the day and even by the hour—where their productivity stands in relation to previous performances and current goals.

Mistakes have a way of sticking in your mind. This is good. It means they will galvanize you into greater feats of assessment and action.

Mistakes have a way of sticking in your mind. This is good. It means they will galvanize you into greater feats of assessment and action. A person without leadership qualities will make a mistake and get bogged down in recrimination and regret. Conversely, the person who knows how to lead will welcome mistakes as learning experiences. What you learn from the mistakes can make you a far better leader in the future.

Impossible Can Be Inside Your Head

In 1833 Cornelius Vanderbilt took a train journey. He hadn't intended to. Vanderbilt owned a highly successful ferry business (hence his nickname "Commodore") and regarded railways as a dangerous newfangled invention.

But he had no other way of reaching his meeting on time, so he boarded the Camden and Amboy Line. In the same car sat the former U.S. president John Quincy Adams. Vanderbilt grumbled the whole way.

En route the axle snapped. The train ran off the track, causing three deaths and several injuries. Having survived America's first fatal train accident, Vanderbilt swore he would henceforth have nothing to do with railroads—a commitment he kept for the next 30 years.

He'd reached his 60s when he grudgingly bought some shares in a railroad venture. For the next 15 years his involvement in the railroad business earned him over $100 million—roughly $20 billion in today's money. He died America's richest man. And all because he had the guts to overcome an old prejudice.

There's nothing like a bad experience to put you off a particular course of action. Never visiting a certain city again. Never buying a certain stock again. Never seeing a certain person again.

> *The option you refuse to consider on the basis of past experience may often emerge as the most profitable one to take.*

Overcoming aversion can take a massive mental effort. Nevertheless, the option you refuse to consider on the basis of past experience may often emerge as the most profitable one to take. Saying "I won't do that again" just because it didn't work last time simply skews your vision and renders you less able to recognize opportunity when it occurs.

Deal with Impossible Relationships

In 1935 my father was a leader at a boys' camp in Michigan. It was in the middle of the Great Depression, and Dad had to watch every penny. One day he filled the car with gasoline to go to a city 15 miles away. But before he got there, the car stalled; it was out of gas. A spike had punctured the gas tank.

It did not take long to identify the culprit—a ten-year-old boy in the camp. I disliked this rich, arrogant boy. I wanted my father to see that the "spoiled brat" was severely disciplined.

Instead, a few hours later, I was appalled and angered to see Dad sitting on the edge of the dock with his arm around the boy, discussing calmly what had happened. He demonstrated love and compassion. And I have reason to believe that the future course of that boy's life was altered for the better because my father turned a serious and expensive problem into an opportunity to do good.

Some of the most challenging problems we face concern relationships. Anyone with a background in the pastorate or marriage counseling will know from direct observation how quickly and inexorably relationships can implode. Husband and wife, parent and child, director and employee—they can all fall out with tragic repercussions.

> *Broken relationships leave a poisonous trail behind them. Influential leaders keep relationships working.*

Are these situations less salvageable than others? No. It's just that most people decide it's easier to back out of relationships than to mend them. But broken relationships leave a poisonous trail behind them. Influential leaders keep relationships working.

When Problems Won't Go Away

In 1950 God blessed our family with a son. But tragedy was soon to follow. During the delivery, the boy was brutalized by a world-famous but intoxicated doctor. Our son, Johnny, lived as an invalid for more than 24 years.

At one level, Johnny's illness presented a constant challenge and a constant drain on our mental and financial resources. At another level, though, the situation opened many new doors.

For example, I never cease to marvel at the way people's perception of me changes when they discover I was the father of a son with cerebral palsy. Up to that point, their view is superficial. They see that I live in a fine house, drive a fine car, jet around the world, meet with leaders, and write books. Consequently, they conclude I cannot possibly understand their problems.

But those who know about Johnny know that my wife and I have experienced the depths of suffering. Also, I cannot express what a blessing Johnny was to me personally. What could have been an overwhelming obstacle became instead a channel of mercy to my own life and ministry.

Influential leaders never attempt to make others feel sorry for them.

Influential leaders never attempt to make others feel sorry for them. When confronting difficulties, they do not complain about "sacrificing themselves for the sake of others." They get on with things and make them work. Making other people feel sorry for us in such situations constitutes a refusal to let difficulty ripen into opportunity.

When the Young Nak Church was established in 1946 with 27 North Korean refugees, it met on a mountain in Seoul. All they had was a threadbare tent. One Sunday the weight of a heavy snowfall caused the tent to collapse. All the members of the church were destitute. Not one of them had money. And yet the young pastor, Dr. Han, suggested they needed a church building. That seemed like an impossibility.

But influential leaders don't counsel their fears. They don't insist that every possible obstacle be overcome before they engage in an enterprise. They determine what needs to be done, they make the decision, and then they seek solutions to the problems. Leaders of faith know that staying power will overcome impossibilities.

One lady in the congregation said she had no money but she would give her wedding ring. Another lady said that other than the clothes she was wearing, her only possession was a quilt she would give to the church fund. She would sleep when the woman with whom she lived was awake and use her quilt. A third woman said that all she had was a spoon and a rice bowl. She gave that. She could borrow her friend's spoon and rice bowl.

The money began to come in. Construction began on a magnificent church edifice. Then in 1950 the Communists came down from the north and pushed the South Koreans nearly into the sea. During the ensuing Korean War, the Communists converted the church into an ammunition depot.

It was almost four years before the members of Dr. Han's church could get back to Seoul to worship in that building. But their return vindicated Dr. Han's visionary decision to go ahead with the project, even at that difficult period in his nation's history.

Summary

Impossibility is opportunity in disguise.

In this chapter, I have emphasized visionary decision making in the face of failure, because most people see failure as the point at which leadership effectiveness ends. Yet influential leaders count failures as assets. Why? Because only failure forces you to go back to basics and think again.

Every decision you make as a leader encapsulates your response to some challenge or obstacle. Visionary decision making allows you to keep your eyes on the objective and not on the things that are going wrong or getting in the way. It takes discipline. And it takes determination.

Influential leaders make mistakes. But they also learn from their mistakes and use them to achieve greater effectiveness. You can never correct a problem if you don't admit that a problem exists. And if mistakes stay uncorrected, they usually multiply and grow worse.

That forces you to take responsibility. Unless you assume responsibility, both for your own mistakes and those of the people in your group, you cannot correct them and profit from them. Never blame other people or adverse circumstances.

Don't hesitate to go to the disaster area and assess the damage. Ask yourself how severe the effects are likely to be and how far they are likely to reach. Discover and eliminate the causes. Mistakes usually result from (1) an error in judgment, (2) poor planning, (3) insufficient information, or (4) defective follow-up. Examine all these areas in depth.

The influential leader does not procrastinate. He or she reevaluates, redirects assets, and starts immediately on corrective action.

DECIDE TO GO FURTHER FASTER

When the French lawyer Nicolas Sarkozy became president of France in 2007, several English language newspapers referred to him as "energetic."

Perhaps the editorial writers had in mind the TV images of Sarkozy jogging in Paris. But energy goes far beyond looking physically fit. Its more important qualities are sheer stamina and the ability to stay ahead of almost everyone on almost everything. And you don't need youth to possess it.

When Deng Xiaoping took over the leadership of China in 1979, he already exceeded retirement age by Western standards. Yet he demonstrated an energy not seen in many men half his age. In his ninetieth year, he was still thinking clearly and refining his vision for the future of his beloved country.

The French leader Napoleon said that he owed his success to youth, health, and the ability to stand physical strain without limit. He had the "power to sleep at any moment" and a stomach which could "digest anything."

The pioneer nurse Florence Nightingale, according to her biographer Edward T. Cook, "stood twenty hours at a stretch, apportioning quarters, distributing stores, directing work, or assisting in operations."

The religious leader John Wesley traveled on horseback the equivalent of ten times around the world's equator. He authored more publications than any writer in the English language—a record surpassed only recently by the American science fiction writer Isaac Asimov. He read books while making his horseback journeys. When he was past 80, he complained that he could not read and work more than 15 hours a day!

One of the most energetic leaders I've ever met was Sir Bruce Small, former chairman of the Haggai Institute (Australia) board of directors. Sir Bruce served simultaneously as a member of Parliament and as mayor of the Gold Coast in Queensland. He also headed the largest property development company in Queensland. He is featured in the *Guinness World Records* books as the oldest man ever to run for an elective office for the first time and win. He was 76 at the time.

Sir Bruce insisted on having his phone number listed. He told me his constituents had a right to get to him when they needed him. His wife, Lady Lillian, told me he hardly ever slept through a night without several emergency telephone calls. His internationally heralded leadership got its thrust from a seemingly limitless energy supply.

It's rare for leaders to reach a position of real influence without having energy.

People get into leadership positions for many reasons—because of popularity, because of connections with the right people, because of intellectual ability, or just because they are in the right place at the right time. But it's rare for leaders to reach a position of real influence without having energy.

The influential leader has taken a visionary decision to work longer hours, read more voluminously, waste less time, and generally live life optimally. He glows with energy. Energy enables the influential leader to make more contacts, write more letters, travel more miles, take in more information, train more people, and make more phone calls than other people do. Study any area of human endeavor, and you will find a correlation between the level of energy and the effectiveness of leadership.

What Energy Is

An influential leader's energy communicates to others through his physical vitality, his mental alertness, his hard work, and his commitment and persistence.

Energy is physical vitality

We all feel attracted to people with physical vitality—those who radiate good health and purposeful activity. Young people, especially, are drawn to those who demonstrate this kind of energy.

> *We all feel attracted to people with physical vitality—those who radiate good health and purposeful activity.*

At the age of 66, Ernest H. Watson assumed the deanship of Haggai Institute, a truly overwhelming responsibility. No one, including me, has matched the hours he invested in the training sessions. For five weeks, he sat through every single lecture. In addition to that, he was available for counsel.

Immediately after his quiet time in the morning, he would plunge into the Olympic-size swimming pool for 50 laps, long before men half his age were out of bed. Between seminar sessions, he would screen applicants, preach, travel, and write extensive reports to the donors who made the program possible.

I remember a man from India coming to me and complaining that the regimen at Haggai Institute was too demanding. He said, "It's inhuman to expect anyone to start the day at seven in the morning and continue until nine at night for five solid weeks."

I asked his age.

"Thirty-six," he replied.

"This year Dr. Watson is twice your age. Have you noticed that he has been at the morning devotions every day, at every meal, at every lecture period, at every tea break? He works past eleven at night, and is often awakened by one of the participants who is sick."

After his training, the young man returned to take up an effective leadership position in India. He confessed that Dr. Watson's energy had made a powerful impact on him.

Demonstrating energy through physical vitality lets others know you are in control.

Demonstrating energy through physical vitality lets others know you are in control. It gives your followers a feeling of confidence and well-being. Physical vitality is a desirable trait, and people follow leaders with characteristics they want to imitate.

When the celebrated clergyman J.C. Massee was in his 90s, he told me; "John, you can have greater insights at my age than you did when you were thirty. You can have a greater understanding of the really important priorities. You can empathize with people much better than in your younger years. But when you lose your physical vitality, something happens. You lose your leadership power because people will not follow a man they perceive to be feeble."

A leader does not require perfect health to draw others to himself. Franklin Delano Roosevelt, for instance, was unable to walk because of polio, but he had boundless energy and physical vitality. He served as U.S. president from 1933 to 1945, longer than anyone else in American history.

Energy is mental alertness

Claude Brown owned a thriving trucking business in Atlanta, Georgia. He made decisions faster than anyone I have ever known. One day I asked him about it.

"Well, John, I have an adequate mind," he said, "and I figure if I am right fifty-one percent of the time, the sheer speed with which I make decisions will put me ahead of the competition." At 67, Claude Brown exuded more energy than many much younger people. His mental alertness made him successful.

Not all leaders are intellectual giants. But all influential leaders have mental alertness and physical vitality. Intelligence supported by a high energy level and governed by good character will guarantee exceptional leadership.

Intelligence supported by a high energy level and governed by good character will guarantee exceptional leadership.

So how does mental alertness make a difference?

- *The leader with mental alertness will observe trends.* He will see big issues and essential details. Observation lays the groundwork for wise action. The best observer constantly questions meanings, motives, and relationships. When World War II ended, Han Kyung Chik was teaching school in North Korea. He observed the large number of children orphaned by the war and recognized the critical need for educational facilities. He grasped the areas of social service required to meet the needs of the people brutalized by war. Out of his keen observation came the leadership philosophy that governed his work for more than 50 years.

- *The leader with mental alertness will have foresight.* When Roald Amundsen made the trip that resulted in the discovery of the South Pole, he took along 97 selected dogs from Alaska. As he proceeded southward over ice barriers, he established supply stations. He marked them so well by signs and flags that when he returned, he never failed to locate them—even when they were hidden in dense fog or covered by fresh snow. His thorough preparation allowed him to trek successfully across 350 miles of ice-covered terrain.

- *The leader with mental alertness will have the opportunity to reflect and reason.* Through reflection and reasoning, the leader penetrates the heart of the profoundest problem. Reflection and reasoning pierce shams, uncover hidden secrets, command respect. They create leaders with incisive drive. They open the gate to personal achievement. I have been blessed by the friendship of two men who, on hearing a plan, can lay bare a weakness in it with explosive speed. If you do not have this ability yourself, strengthen your leadership by making yourself vulnerable to the criticism of colleagues who have that gift. It will spare you some costly errors.

Energy is hard work

Work is the most visible output of human energy.

No sluggard ever excelled as a leader.

No sluggard ever excelled as a leader. When John Wanamaker was postmaster general of the United States, he stunned Washington society by going to work at seven thirty every morning, two and half hours earlier than official Washington. In 1920, when he was 82 years old,

Wanamaker was at his office in Philadelphia from eight in the morning until six in the evening.

Since 1941, I have made it a point to interview men and women I consider outstanding leaders. Without exception, when I ask the secret of their success, they include somewhere in their response the words *energy* and *work*.

Horace Mann was a remarkable person. Until he was 15 he never attended school more than ten weeks in a year. But when he was 20 he prepared himself so thoroughly that in a mere six months he was admitted to the sophomore class at Brown University. He graduated with highest honors three years later.

Mann practiced law, returned to the University to teach Latin and Greek and serve as librarian, and then took an interest in public affairs. After serving in the Massachusetts legislature, he became secretary of the Board of Education. He made the educational program in Massachusetts the prototype for the rest of the United States. At 52, Mann became a U.S. congressman and then president of Antioch College in Ohio.

"Be ashamed to die until you have
won some victory for humanity."

His last words to students, delivered in a baccalaureate address just a few weeks before his death, were: "Be ashamed to die until you have won some victory for humanity." Often people asked how he had succeeded in his numerous projects. His consistent reply was, "In almost every case, it has required constant, hard, conscientious work. I consider there is no permanent success possible without hard and severe work, coupled with the highest and most praiseworthy aims."

I often chuckle at union leaders who put in a 60-, 70-, and even 80-hour week trying to win a 32-hour week for the union members. Could that be why the union leader is a leader—and the members are not?

Energy is commitment and persistence

The inventor Thomas Edison used to say that 99 percent of genius was sheer dogged persistence.

In 1878, Edison predicted that he would one day light homes and offices with electricity. "When it is known how I have accomplished my object, everyone will wonder why they've never thought of it," he said. At that point, Edison had not yet invented the electric light bulb. He had many obstacles to overcome before he accomplished his goal. But he believed he could do it. He had commitment and persistence.

It took thousands of experiments to find the right material for the filament of the bulb. He tried every substance he could think of (including platinum, beard hair, and lamp black). Finally, he succeeded with carbonized cotton thread. Edison's commitment and incredible persistence gave the world the electric light bulb. At the time of its invention, it was considered a miracle.

Commitment and persistence require a tremendous amount of physical, intellectual, and emotional energy. You must believe in and work toward your goal against all odds. You must do the tasks no one else will do.

Bob Pierce, founder of World Vision, made a huge impact across Asia. Shortly before his death, Pierce told me, "I honestly believe that God intended another man to do what I finally did." He mentioned the other man's name. "But he wouldn't make the kind of total commitment necessary to achieve it. He was too lazy to lead. And so God took me, despite my lesser gifts, and used me instead. I was willing to commit everything to the accomplishment of that goal."

Pierce's energy was phenomenal. He made his last journey around the world as an advanced cancer victim. He was confined to a wheelchair. To the end, he maintained his original commitment to help those in need.

The European playwright Henrik Ibsen said, "The greatest of men is he who most stands alone." And the car manufacturer Henry Ford disclosed a similar spirit when he said, "I refuse to recognize any impossibilities."

American president Woodrow Wilson told his opponents, "You can turn aside from the measure if you like. You can decline to follow me. You can deprive me of office and turn away from me. But you cannot drive me from power as long as I steadfastly stand for what I believe to be the interests and the legitimate demands of the people themselves."

Commitment and persistence will let you overcome opposition and persecution. The apostle Paul tells of the opposition he received:

> In labors more abundant, in stripes above measure, in prisons more frequently, in deaths often. From the Jews five times I received forty stripes minus one. Three times I was beaten with rods; once I was stoned; three times I was shipwrecked; a night and a day I have been in the deep; in journeys often, in perils of waters, in perils of robbers, in perils of my own countrymen, in perils of the Gentiles, in perils in the city, in perils in the wilderness, in perils in the sea, in perils among false brethren; in weariness and toil, in sleeplessness often, in hunger and thirst, in fastings often, in cold and nakedness—besides the other things, what comes upon me daily: my deep concern for all the churches (2 Corinthians 11:23-28).

And yet in spite of the opposition and persecution he received, Paul was able to say, "I have fought the good fight, I have finished the race, I have kept the faith" (2 Timothy 4:7). Endurance impregnated his leadership with vitality. That took energy.

Visionary Decisions to Help You Go Further Faster

We are challenged by the energy of leaders such as Napoleon, Florence Nightingale, John Wesley, or Ernest Watson. Leadership requires physical vitality, mental alertness, hard work, commitment, and persistence.

> *Some people naturally possess greater energy than others. Nevertheless, you can increase your energy level.*

Some people naturally possess greater energy than others. Nevertheless, you can increase your energy level. Many things sap your strength and deplete your energy. Being overweight, getting insufficient exercise, having poor sleeping habits, suffering depression and stress—all these can make you less effective by reducing the energy you have available for leadership.

Resolve to take these visionary decisions to help you raise your energy level.

1. Go further faster by giving yourself the right gasoline

Diet impacts your energy level. A friend returned from a three-week vacation with her family. In that time, she had eaten mostly fast food. She felt sluggish, her joints ached, and she couldn't sleep. Her energy level was very low. By changing her diet, she was able to restore her energy, feel younger, sleep better, and get rid of her pains.

How do you eat right for maximum energy? According to Dr. Kenneth H. Cooper, the world's leading authority on total wellness, the secret lies in balance—balance in *when* you eat and balance in *what* you eat.[22] In many parts of the world, people eat too much at the last meal of the day. The proper balance is:

- 25 percent of your calorie intake in the morning
- 50 percent at noon
- 25 percent in the evening

In addition, you should balance the three major food types: 50 percent complex carbohydrates, 20 percent protein, and 30 percent fats.

Healthy eating, according to dietary specialist Nathan Pritikin, "will enhance the acuity of all your senses, give you boundless new energy, take away that tired feeling, and may even reduce your daily sleep requirement. Some symptoms of aging even disappear."[23]

Pritikin's program recommends restricting consumption of salt, alcohol, and high-caffeine beverages such as coffee and tea. Salt contributes to hypertension. Alcohol damages the liver and destroys brain function. Caffeine increases the heart rate and contributes to hypertension.

Eating right involves more than going on a diet for a week or two. You must change the way you think about food, especially where processed foods are becoming the norm. Ironically, in "advanced" countries some of the most popular foods are damaging to health. But if you develop eating habits in line with the best medical advice, you will live longer, feel healthier, and look better.

And you will also have more energy.

2. Go further faster by getting your body working

Countless studies show that a regular program of exercise increases energy, producing a healthy body and a long life.

Boredom produces fatigue,
and work produces energy.

In *How Never to Be Tired*, a gem of a book I've returned to many times, Marie Beynon Rae claims the answer to fatigue is not rest but work.[24] She insists that boredom produces fatigue, and work produces energy. I have found this true. When my workload has deprived me of sleep, I have restored my energy more effectively by exercising for half an hour than by sleeping.

The best kind of exercise increases your heartbeat for at least 30 minutes a day. Walking, running, cycling, and swimming are excellent forms of exercise. Isometric exercise such as weight lifting is useful for building muscle tissue and bone density, but it should not substitute for exercises that increase your heart rate.

Exercise benefits your health if you do it regularly. So schedule it into your day. Make it a priority. Your increased health, feeling of well-being, and added energy will make the time commitment worthwhile.

3. Go further faster by keeping a positive mental attitude

Increased energy comes not just from conditioning your body through proper eating, exercise, and plenty of sleep, but also from conditioning your mind through developing positive attitudes and eliminating negative emotions. Your body provides you with your storehouse of energy. Your attitude decides how much of that energy you release.

Do you know people who have a hard time getting up in the morning? Are any of them zealous fishermen? On a work day, they have a hard time getting out of bed by six or seven o'clock. But if they are going fishing, they set the alarm for four in order to meet their friends at four thirty. A few minutes before four, they are wide awake!

They hook up the trailer, they pull the boat to the river, they slide it down the landing jetty, and they get wet. They use more energy over the next 15 hours than they have during the preceding three weeks of work. If they are successful in catching a lot of fish, they come back feeling better than they have felt in weeks. They seem aglow with energy. What makes the difference? Attitude!

If you want to be energetic, act energetic.

If you want to be energetic, act energetic. Energy for leadership will come if you are as interested in people as you are in your leisure activities.

4. Go further faster by mercilessly eliminating negative emotions

Nothing will divert your energy from constructive leadership faster than negative emotions. They will direct your energy into nonproductive channels. There are many negative emotions, and influential leaders learn how to deal with them in constructive ways:

- *Anger.* Do you repress anger? Anger has positive functions, but if handled incorrectly it produces stress, ulcers, and hypertension. You can waste a lot of energy needlessly by either repressing or nurturing anger. Instead, recognize your anger, analyze why you are angry, make changes where possible to relieve your anger, and accept the situation if changes cannot be made.

- *Hatred and bitterness.* These negative emotions are always wrong. They are mental and physical poisons that will destroy you if you let them. Hatred and bitterness may appear to generate a lot of energy. But in reality, they only divert energy from constructive to destructive purposes. Usually this harms both the hated person and the person doing the hating. Frankly, only love can overcome hatred and bitterness. These words of Jesus contain a good deal of psychological wisdom: "I say to you, love your enemies, bless those who curse you, do good to those who hate you, and pray for those who spitefully use you and persecute you" (Matthew 5:43-44).

The route to winning over anxiety lies in careful focusing on your vision and goals.

- *Anxiety.* This general sense of uneasiness or discomfort differs from fear in that it has no specific object or cause. This vagueness makes anxiety difficult to deal with. Focusing one's attention on anxieties leaves little energy for constructive accomplishments—precisely the things that would help relieve anxiety. The route to winning over anxiety lies in careful focusing on your vision and goals.

- *Fear.* This can be useful or destructive, depending on the situation. Like all emotions, fear produces energy. If someone approaches you with a knife, you will experience fear. That fear will give you the energy to turn and run faster than you ever thought possible. Fears that are phobias—exaggerated and irrational fears— also generate energy, but they turn energy away from constructive purposes. The fear of the dark, of heights, of closed places, of speaking before a crowd—these inhibit your development as a leader. The first step to overcoming your fears? Identify them and study them. Something brought into the light of understanding will lose much of its power.

Summary

Going further faster is a question of energy.

Energy attracts attention. Energy attracts followers. The leader who demonstrates enthusiasm and energy will gain the acceptance and confidence of others. Energy conveys the ideas of authority, of excitement, of success, and of purposeful activity. The dictionaries define it as "the vigorous exertion of power" and "the capacity of acting or being active."

The leader demonstrates energy in a variety of ways. Vitality is crucial. Even if advanced in years or suffering a physical handicap, the influential leader radiates well-being and purposeful activity. Even without being an intellectual giant, he will use his mind to its fullest capacity for observation, foresight, and reflection and reasoning. He will enjoy working hard in pursuit of his vision and will demonstrate commitment and perseverance when times are tough.

Some people possess much natural energy. Others have less. But your energy level can always increase. All it takes is visionary decision making to eat well, exercise regularly, maintain a positive mental attitude, and eliminate negative emotions.

DECIDE TO BE THERE AT THE END

Sustainability counts for leaders as well as companies. Just like companies, leaders go through lean times and downturns. And like companies, they either meet the challenge and thrive—or they fold.

Let me speak from experience.

After some fruitful years in the pastorate, I moved into itinerant evangelism. I did this with great reluctance. Our only child had been victimized by cerebral palsy from birth. I didn't feel right being away unless it was absolutely necessary. Johnny needed me; so did my wife, Christine.

In the end I received 420 unsolicited invitations—to conduct evangelistic campaigns, preaching missions, evangelistic Bible teaching seminars—before I felt a bedrock conviction that God wanted me to move.

Almost immediately I ran into opposition from a ministry in the same field. To spare their embarrassment, I will call them Gospel Enterprise.

The first clue came in the 1960s when a friend of one of my associates sat in on the annual board meeting of Gospel Enterprise. He heard one of its executives say, "Haggai is the only one we haven't been able to sweep under our umbrella."

Not long after, I was asked to conduct an evangelistic meeting in Lisbon, Portugal. Never in the history of Portugal, which was 99 percent Catholic, had a Protestant minister been invited to conduct meetings in a public venue.

No sooner had the planning for the Lisbon meetings begun than two executives of Gospel Enterprise flew to Lisbon to see our Portuguese committee chairman. The chairman told me later that they damned my ministry with faint praise, and then concluded, "Haggai won't make much of a difference. But surely he can't hurt anything. We'll plan to come at a later date for a history-making evangelistic effort. You may just want to wait for us."

The Lisbon leadership declined their offer.

Next, a friend of Gospel Enterprise, a missionary to Portugal and a good man, used his influence to stonewall our efforts. This surprised me because he had cooperated with us enthusiastically two years earlier. Only toward the end of the event, after thousands had made decisions for Christ, did he tell me he'd been acting on instructions from Gospel Enterprise.

---

*I asked God for the grace to stay true
to Him and to the vision He had given me.*

Their opposition intensified to such a degree that the founder of World Vision, Bob Pierce, flew from Dacca, Bangladesh, specifically to warn me that "Gospel Enterprise is out to stop you." He advised me to watch out; he didn't want to see the ministry hurt.

The opposition in Portugal wasn't an isolated incident. On several occasions the leaders of Gospel Enterprise attempted to cancel my engagements. Sometimes they intervened directly, as when they torpedoed a city-wide series of meetings in Honolulu that the clergy had asked me to consider.

These events still sadden me. I didn't understand it then, and I don't understand it now. But I asked God for the grace to stay true to Him and to the vision He had given me.

Thank God for Opposition

Sustainability for leaders demands more than physical stamina. It draws upon a mental toughness, a visionary decision to put aside the demands of personal comfort, and even, where necessary, of loved ones in order to see the vision realized.

Recently I paid a visit to the cofounder of Amway, Rich DeVos.

He told me he and his lifelong business partner, Jay Van Andel, first met in high school. They started their partnership just after the Second World War with $700.

With a bank loan, they bought a Piper Cub and started a flying school. The G.I. Bill provided funds for training, and they saw the approaching rise in demand for flying skills. They didn't know how to fly, but they didn't have to; they simply hired instructors. Later, as G.I. Bill funding was phased out, they sold the business and moved on—first as distributors for Nutrilite, then as founders of the venture that became Amway.

DeVos's career has been punctuated by what he calls "wars"—periods of determined opposition from, among others, the FDA and the Canadian government. On several occasions this opposition could have put him out of business. He has suffered considerable misrepresentation in the media. But he's won through integrity and persistence. His globe-girdling business today ranks as a modern-day super success story.

Those who want an easy ride or who retreat at the first sign of trouble will never become influential leaders.

If you want to survive downturns in the market and make the most of your opportunities, you will need mental toughness. If you want to weather personal challenges and difficult relationships, you will need mental toughness. Those who want an easy ride or who retreat at the first sign of trouble will never become influential leaders, in business or anywhere else.

In my more than 60 years in the ministry across the globe, touching every continent, I have so often heard leaders say, "We need to back off of this project. God must not be in it. So much opposition has arisen, it prohibits the possibility of advance."

I wonder what Bible they're reading from—what version, what language? I do not find any place in Scripture where God did a great work that escaped virulent opposition.

Will Houghton, president of a leading American college, suffered severe headaches. And yet, most of us who knew Dr. Houghton had no idea of his illness. He did not speak of his great problem. His humor could put at ease the students who would tense up in his commanding presence. This man, who demonstrated unique leadership until his death in 1946, pursued his work with a staying power that continues to challenge me today.

Why Sustainability Builds Leadership

Sustainability means managing desire

William Borden of the famous Borden family in America graduated from Yale University in 1909. While he was a student, cars were just beginning to come on the streets. One day he was looking out the window and admired a car. His roommate said, "Bill, why don't you buy one? You have the money."

But Borden had different priorities. He had committed his life and his money to achieve those priorities, and nothing—not even the lure of a new automobile—was going to change his plans. His staying power overcame personal desire.

*"Efficiency is the willingness to sacrifice
personal desires to the will to win."*

Thirty years ago, I read a line that has stuck with me: "Efficiency is the willingness to sacrifice personal desires to the will to win."

Every leader has experienced moments when it seems preferable to abandon a project, give in to the detractors, or take the easy road. Also, a leader will frequently face the opportunity to satisfy a personal desire that, though not bad in itself, nevertheless interferes with the accomplishment of his goals. Remember, the will to win must come first. And that takes sustainability.

Sustainability means no bailing out

Many have demonstrated outstanding leadership by practicing sustainability in the face of financial limitations.

George Müller, who founded homes for orphans in Bristol, England, changed the lives of thousands of children and made a positive impact on England by his compassionate care. Many times he did not have money to supply the children's next meal. He never complained. He never whimpered. He never threatened to discontinue his ministry to the orphans. He worked by faith. What made Müller unique was his staying power.

*Many in positions of leadership today
lack the mental toughness of the influential
leader and quickly bail out under pressure.*

Sustainability rests on a deep commitment to vision. Many in positions of leadership today lack the mental toughness of the influential leader and quickly bail out under pressure. When you talk with them intimately, you discover they have already made plans to abandon their leadership position.

In other words, they are committed to organizational goals only if they can reach those goals at minimal personal cost. They are weak leaders, easily intimidated and forced to back down. They program themselves for failure.

Sustainability means focus

We think of sustainability as an asset useful in bad times. In fact, though, the greatest challenges to staying power arise through prosperity and easy living.

Note this paradox. If you ask most business leaders what their motivation is, eventually they will say, "To make money." And if you ask why they want to make money, in most cases they will say things like, "So I can drive a better car, have a nicer house, afford schooling for my children, go on more expensive holidays, and retire in financial security."

Motivations tied to personal comfort lack reliability.

But motivations tied to personal comfort lack reliability. When times are hard, you may feel that persevering puts you further away from such goals, not closer to them. Conversely, when times are easy, you attain your desired level of comfort—and lose motivation.

John D. Rockefeller, the Standard Oil tycoon and the world's richest man in his time, had little interest in wealth per se. While other millionaires' children took luxury for granted, Rockefeller insisted that his family operate on a tight budget, mending worn clothes rather than buying new ones.

I believe that national wealth can constitute a serious disadvantage to a country. During the Cold War, a powerful orator and a good friend of mine once said, "Russia will never bury America. America will bury itself—unless Americans can break the stranglehold of self-indulgence, wanton waste, and narcissism."

In the light of later economic difficulties, his words have proven prophetic. But the same could have been said of many countries, not only in the West but even in the East, where the preoccupation with status and personal comfort increasingly saps populations of character and values of permanence.

Sustainability means personal resolve

Not every leader can count on the support of family. Leadership is a 24-hour, 7-day-a-week job. It requires doing unpleasant tasks as well as enjoyable ones. Members of a leader's family can easily feel they are taking second place.

David Livingstone, who opened much of Africa for European exploration, was a man of many parts—missionary, writer, cartographer, and anthropologist. But his wife, Mary, gave him constant trouble, always complaining and criticizing. She made his work almost impossible.

The demands on Livingstone were great. In that day, there were no jet airplanes. He could not visit a city a thousand miles away and get back home the same day. The tension became so great that Livingstone sent his wife home to England for more than 12 years, while he suffered and ultimately died in service to the Africans.

The leader fixes his eyes on his mission
and does not let opposition move him from
the path of accomplishing that mission.

The influential leader does not neglect family responsibilities or use work as a way of escaping from difficult relationships at home. But the tensions that often arise between work and home will not be handled successfully without staying power. The leader fixes his eyes on his mission and does not let opposition move him from the path of accomplishing that mission—even opposition from his own family.

Sustainability means sticking with your vision

Sometimes others in the group don't grasp the vision with the same clarity as the leader. They can't see its relevance. Or they don't make vital connections between different parts of the picture. Or they just won't make the effort to help make the vision a reality.

In these situations, the leader feels an urge to gear down to the level of his group. This is a mistake. As leader, you must have a sustainability that refuses to see the vision altered or diluted. If you don't take the vision seriously, nobody else will either. Often, the group members around you will have invested less in the vision than you have; they will rely on your passion to carry them along. You need to interpret events for them, keep clarifying the vision, and face down opposition to insure the success of the enterprise.

Many things can weaken your determination. Illness, distraction, financial limitation, difficult family relationships, betrayal, misunderstanding—all these can make it difficult to stay on track for your organizational goals.

But all these problems have solutions. The difference between staying afloat and going under often lies in your staying power. If you give up, you have already failed. But if you practice sustainability, you will see great opportunities even in seemingly impossible situations.

Visionary Decisions to Help You Be There at the End

Most leaders of any worth have faced times of crisis. The famous preacher Charles Haddon Spurgeon resigned 32 times during his London ministry.

---

*Most leaders of any worth
have faced times of crisis.*

I know what it means to put everything on the line for what you believe in. In the early days of the ministry, I cashed in assets most people regard as off limits—I sold my car, used up my personal savings, borrowed money. I almost lost my house. I do not sit in a comfortable ivory tower to tell you that pursuing a vision can demand the utmost in stamina and determination.

Before crisis moments hit, resolve to make visionary decisions that will build your sustainability.

1. Be there at the end by remembering your vision

Your leadership began with a vision. You had a clear picture of what your group could be or do. You saw how you could move the group toward goals of beneficial permanence that would fulfill the group's real needs. The vision you had was valid when you started, and the need was real. The goals were worthy ones. You can maintain your staying power by remembering your vision and renewing your commitment to it. Doing that will put your current problems in proper perspective.

2. Be there at the end by focusing on your goals

Goals resemble staircases. You've established a set of goals with a certain destination in mind. But operationally the important step is the one you're making right now, not what lies further up. So solve today's challenges today. Leave tomorrow's challenges for tomorrow. Start by focusing on one or two manageable objectives confronting you here and now. Progress on immediate tasks will give your leadership sustainability.

3. Be there at the end by visualizing the future

I have noticed that leaders frequently talk as if the goals they set have already been reached. The president of a retail chain may tell you about his new stores—how much business they do, where they are located—long before the first one has even opened.

Solve today's challenges today.
Leave tomorrow's challenges for tomorrow.

He's not lying. Influential leaders visualize their goals being accomplished. They make the vision a reality in their own minds. So the president will set new goals as if the stores were fully operational.

The late Max Stoffel of Liechtenstein, whose Stoffel linens are known around the world, visualized his goals in precisely this way. He told me that every morning he would get a cup of coffee, return to bed, prop himself up on some pillows, and then, in a state of complete relaxation, mentally rehearse his plans for the day. If he had some appointments, he would rehearse the opening words, what the tone of the conversation would be, what expression he would wear.

He said, "I attribute much of my success to this. When I take up my day's activities, I am simply replaying the role I have already rehearsed. It relieves a lot of pressure and dissipates a lot of stress."

4. Be there at the end by knowing how to relax

Stress undermines sustainability. Most outstanding leaders know how to relax. They understand and practice the habit of solitude. They know how to spend time with their own thoughts, plans, and dreams.

Most outstanding leaders understand
and practice the habit of solitude.

You can do this quite effectively even in crowded situations. One of my associates used to spend two hours a day commuting by bus to work in New York City. Moving to another part of the country reduced his commuting time to less than half an hour by car. But he told me he missed the bus ride, because that was a time when he could relax, commune with God, and review his vision and goals.

5. Be there at the end by devouring biographies

Biographies of great people will strengthen your staying power because they let you see how other great men and women have succeeded. Focus on the truly great achievers. Don't limit yourself to business, but select those whose leadership qualities have distinguished them in other fields, such as politics, sports, or warfare. Inhabit their worlds. Find out what motivated them, how they solved the problems that are common to all human beings, and what, finally, made them great. An honest and insightful biography will give you a rich education.

And Don't Let It Get to You

Gospel Enterprise's attempts to undermine my ministry worked unspeakable hardship on us. In the early days, I went through all my savings, sold my car, and borrowed money to keep the ministry afloat. Each time Gospel Enterprise got our meetings cancelled, we would lose all the money we had put into the preparation—money we would have expected to recoup from the host churches.

On four different occasions we faced bankruptcy and closure. Perhaps the leadership of Gospel Enterprise honestly believed we lacked the qualifications to work in the field of campaign evangelism. But in that case why did they also plagiarize our materials? One magazine article they published copied us almost word for word.

I can tell you honestly, I rejoice in the great good Gospel Enterprise does and in its commitment to reach people for Christ. The fact that it has opposed our ministry can't negate that. Even though it caused us no end of grief and difficulty, God has used Gospel Enterprise to touch thousands of lives.

Today, many individuals in Gospel Enterprise not only commend the work of Haggai Institute, but several support it with their money as well as their prayers.

We took a visionary decision to stand firm, and by God's grace we made it through.

Whatever the motives of the organization's leaders, their opposition made me and those who worked with me stronger. We took a visionary decision to stand firm, and by God's grace we made it through.

The Bonus Achievements

It's a well-known adage that you don't always get what you bargained for. Similarly, your life achievements may yield a bonus beyond the vision you originally set out with. But without doubt, nothing at all will result if you give up half way.

Christopher Columbus had a vision almost nobody else would share. If the earth was round, he reasoned, it meant he could reach Asia by sailing west instead of east and open up a possibly lucrative new trade route. All he had to do was prove it.

First, though, he needed someone to finance the expedition.

He tried John II, king of Portugal, without success, and then the count of Medinaceli in Spain. The count encouraged Columbus for two years, but never actually provided him with the money and supplies he needed. Columbus then contacted Ferdinand and Isabella, king and queen of Castile in Spain. The queen appointed a committee to assess his plans.

Columbus didn't give up. He believed in his mission, and he was determined to hold out for high terms.

Persuading the committee was far from easy. But Columbus didn't give up. He believed in his mission, and he was determined to hold out for high terms. He asked for immediate commission as an admiral. He also sought to become viceroy of all the lands he should discover, receiving one-tenth of all the precious metals mined there.

Though these terms were rejected at first, Queen Isabella finally changed her mind and agreed to the explorer's conditions.

Next he had to find crews for the ships. This seemed almost impossible, in spite of an indemnity offered to criminals and "broken men" who might serve on the expedition. But Columbus again demonstrated his tenacity, and finally three ships, the *Niña*, the *Pinta*, and the *Santa Maria*, set sail on 3 August 1492.

Three days later, the *Pinta* lost its rudder. They had to repair the vessel quickly and secretly, because three Portuguese ships were trying to intercept them. The voyage was punctuated by unrest, with the crews reaching the point of mutiny more than once. It took them until 12 October to reach land.

It wasn't the Far East. And Columbus never did visit the Grand Khan of Cathay as he had hoped. But he did discover two new continents and became one of most famous names in the history books.

Summary

If you are a leader, you will experience pressures and problems that can make you question your vision and contemplate giving up.

But persistence plays a vital role in success. The leader has to hang in there. Leaders who face setbacks in their earliest days often have the mental toughness to win through difficulties later.

To be there at the end, all influential leaders require is determination.

To be there at the end, influential leaders do not need education, charm, family ties, powerful friends, staff, equipment, materials, prestige, or anything else. All they require is determination.

Sustainability overcomes problems. It can thwart illness, personal desire, financial limitations, and the numbing effects of prosperity, family opposition, and betrayal by colleagues.

Many leaders at some time question whether they ought to quit. When those moments hit, leaders can strengthen their sustainability by remembering their vision, by focusing on their goals, by visualization, by relaxation, and by reading about other influential leaders who have achieved what they aimed for.

Sustainability assures success.

DECIDE TO LEAD WITH EFFORTLESS GRACE

For years I admired an insurance salesman named Ben Feldman. Feldman had broken every sales record in insurance history. Yet he lived in a small city in Ohio, not in a metropolitan center. At that time, he sold more insurance than 70 percent of the insurance companies in the United States.

When I arrived home from the office one evening, my wife, Christine, knowing of my fascination with Feldman, said, "Ben Feldman was just on television."

"What does he look like?" I asked, thinking he would have an impressive physique, a compelling voice, and good looks.

"He is short and somewhat overweight," she said. "He is not what you would call handsome. He is certainly not imposing. Nor is his speech impressive."

"Then I wonder what the secret of his success is?"

"The camera went on his eyes," she said. "When you saw his eyes you could understand his success. They conveyed an authority hard to describe. It was indefinable, but it was there."

Afterward, I met Ben Feldman on two occasions. He was gracious and respectful. Although not physically impressive, he had a quiet authority of manner that nearly knocked you over. This did not spring from an aggressive personality. He spoke softly. But his assurance and authority were unmistakable.

Lord of the Flies, a novel by the English author William Golding, tells the story of a group of schoolboys stranded on an island after a plane crash. No grown-ups survive—only the children. The boys all meet on a beach, wondering how they can ensure a rescue.

One of the first things they do is vote for a chief. Two boys vie for the position. Golding tells us that "the most obvious leader was Jack. But there was a stillness about Ralph as he sat there that marked him out."[25]

The rest of the story centers on the leadership struggle between Ralph and Jack. Other boys in the group defer to both as leaders. But while Jack offers excitement and often resorts to force, it is Ralph to whom the other boys feel an instinctive loyalty.

In the nineteenth century, one of America's most influential men was Charles G. Finney, a lawyer of great intellect and scholarship. After his conversion to Christianity, he became an evangelist. He had no entourage, no press corps, no public relations advance team, no public address system. Yet during one six-week period, his preaching resulted in 30,000 becoming Christians.

Authority is an inner quality.
Influential leaders possess it regardless
of their job or position in society.

Even Finney's most vigorous detractors grudgingly admitted he had an air of authority about him. He commanded attention and respect. One time he walked into a textile mill in New York state. Before he was introduced, before he had said a word, all eyes turned toward him. The entire work force listened to everything he said. He had an authority that captured their attention.

Ben Feldman had that quality. The fictional Ralph had it. The former

British prime minister Margaret Thatcher had it. So did the Indian leader Mahatma Gandhi. Something in the demeanor of these leaders communicated to others that they were capable and trustworthy. Not everyone liked them; but everyone took them seriously.

Authority Does Not Equal Power

Authority is an inner quality. Influential leaders possess it regardless of their job or position in society. It enables them to command the respect of others and motivates others to accept their leadership. It does not depend on any external factors. You can have exclusive club memberships, outstanding pedigree, high office, and good looks—and still lack the authority essential to influential leadership.

By contrast, power rests exclusively on these externals. Power holders exert influence only by virtue of their position. There is no such thing as an intrinsically powerful person. You possess power as a CEO or a general or a senator for exactly as long as you hold your rank and position. Unplugged from the organization that appointed you, and relieved of your status privileges, you have no power at all.

Having authority and liking to hold power are two quite different things. Power holders enjoy dominating others. In some cases they may regard this as more important than discharging the duties of their office.

> *You can hold your nation's highest office*
> *and still not be a true leader.*

For this reason they do not always command respect. Having a fast car or running a big company doesn't make other people like you or trust you or want to do what you say. Holding power won't help you exert special influence to move a group toward goals of beneficial permanence that fulfill the group's real needs. Probably that won't interest you anyway. As noted at the beginning of this book, you can hold your nation's highest office and still not be a true leader.

Influential leaders never seek power or enjoy it for its own sake. Not infrequently they find power thrust upon them by a populace that instinctively recognizes their worth in leadership. Even so they may not always accept it.

When Sun Yat-sen, founder of China's nationalist party, returned to his homeland after the Wuhan rising in 1911, he did something almost unheard of. Realizing he would not command wide support as president of the nation, he voluntarily handed over the office to another man, Yuan Shikai. Outer authority did not matter to him. He gave it away. Yet even as he did so, the people recognized him as the nation's true leader. His authority was unassailable.

Jesus Christ did not have wealth,
a large house, or social status, yet
He commanded immediate respect.

As one would expect, Jesus Christ possessed authority in abundance. The Gospels do not tell us He had a commanding physical presence. He did not have wealth, a large house, or social status. By the world's standards, He was not a success. And yet He commanded immediate respect; those around Him hungered to hear what He had to say.

At the time of Jesus, one of the 70 most important Jewish people in Judea was a man named Nicodemus. He belonged to the ruling committee called the Sanhedrin. He observed his religion meticulously. He knew 400 ceremonial laws by heart, fasted two days a week, and prayed four times a day. In comparison, Jesus held no formal rank and possessed no official status. Undoubtedly, Nicodemus was older than Jesus. And yet, when the two met, Nicodemus began by addressing Jesus as "Rabbi," meaning "Teacher." Jesus possessed an authority that no one, not even His detractors, denied.

In the business arena, one of the men most noted for his authority was the businessman and millionaire John D. Rockefeller. Rockefeller owned 30 percent of the stock of Standard Oil, then America's largest and most successful company. He was the consummate business strategist. And yet he never felt the need to impose himself on his colleagues.

One opponent recalls a particularly heated meeting with Rockefeller and some members of the Standard Oil board:

> Everybody talked except Mr. Rockefeller. He sat in a rocking chair, softly swinging back and forth, his hands over his face. I got pretty excited…and I made a speech which, I guess, was pretty warlike. Well, right in the middle of it, John Rockefeller stopped rocking and took down his hands and looked at me. You never saw such eyes. He took me all in, saw just how much fight he could expect from me, and I knew it, and then up went his hands and back and forth went his chair.[26]

The Yugoslavian Nun

Born in Skopje, Macedonia, in 1910, the daughter of an Albanian grocer, Agnes Gonxha Bojaxhiu was called to the life of the convent at the age of 12. She became one of the Sisters of Loreto and a missionary in eastern India. In 1946, she received a second call, this time to leave the convent and live among the poor.

One of her first projects was a home for dying destitutes in Calcutta. Here the homeless and forsaken could die in peace, knowing love and tenderness. This project led to others: an orphanage for abandoned children, a colony for lepers, a home for the elderly, a workshop for the unemployed, and a free-lunch program. Today, the Missionaries of Charity minister to the sick, dying, and destitute in 31 countries.

Gonxha Bojaxhiu—better known as Mother Teresa of Calcutta—systematically shunned all extravagance. She owned only two changes of clothing. When a supporter gave her an expensive car—a white Lincoln Continental convertible with red leather seats—she auctioned it off to benefit the poor. Her office contained only a single telephone line, and for a while she doubted whether even that was necessary. She traveled third class on trains. Her organization had no public relations officials and kept a low profile.

> *Without anything we would recognize as power, Mother Teresa founded an order of dedicated nuns and brothers who now work on five continents.*

Without anything we would recognize as power, Mother Teresa founded an order of dedicated nuns and brothers who now work on five continents. She became an international symbol of goodness, honored by political leaders across the world. In 1979, she received the Nobel Peace Prize because "the loneliest, the most wretched, and the dying... have at her hands received compassion without condescension."

The $192,000 she received went to build a leprosarium in India.

The Weakness of Power

General Samson Tucay directs the Police National Training Institute in the Philippines. He runs 20 fully staffed facilities, with a brief to train all 110,000 Philippine National Police (PNP) officers and all new recruits.

Since 2004, however, this Haggai Institute graduate has pioneered a far more extraordinary program based in the old U.S. military base at Subic Bay. It caters solely for the police "scalawags"—corrupt officers on the brink of dismissal.

Says Tucay, "Before they are yanked out of the service, I get them out here in isolation training, and I try to join hands with them and bring them back to the force."

More than 2000 officers have come through Subic Bay. And Tucay's determination to continue the program, and its striking success, go back to a bitter personal experience.

"I was a monster myself as a result of all the police training that I received," he admits. "This shattered my human dignity and put a lot of hatred in my heart. It turned me into an arrogant, rogue cop."

All military organizations have rigid hierarchies. Everyone knows his place, and everyone knows everyone else's place. This helps the fighting unit remain effective in battle conditions. Importantly, obedience to commands does not depend on the leadership qualities of the officers, though many are fine leaders. Indeed, the structure is designed to keep functioning even if the leaders show little intelligence or strength of character.

---

*Bereft of real authority, power
structures inevitably decay.*

But bereft of real authority, power structures inevitably decay. In Tucay's case, the power structure of the PNP had decayed to the point of allowing abusive behavior to filter down from one rank to the next. Someone had to intervene.

Tucay's answer was to remove from his trainees all symbols of power—cell phones, watches, even visits from relatives. They are awakened at four o'clock every morning and made to undergo rigorous physical exercise that lasts almost unbroken until eight thirty in the evening.

But even as he removes the trappings of power and position, Tucay ensures that his staff set strong personal examples of authority.

"The training is very hard," he says, "but they do not hear any shouts from us, they do not hear any invectives from us, no punishments. In all the hard physical activities we go through, we join them. We eat the same food they eat. We sleep on the same uncomfortable beds they sleep on. We just tell them there is a purpose in their being here with us, and that purpose is God's purpose—for them to accept God in their lives and endeavor to live that acceptance going forward."

Tucay's experience illustrates the kind of problem that arises where power exists without personal authority. Inability to win the respect of others deprived many PNP officers of the legitimacy their rank deserved.

The Business Army

Business people do not wear stripes to indicate rank. But they may devise other ways of communicating status. A key to the executive washroom, a private parking place, a Savile Row suit, a second secretary, and a large salary are among the many things that symbolize power in the business world.

In his insightful book, *Power: How to Get It, How to Use It*, Michael Korda describes the symbolic value of a limousine: "Rented limousines are less prestigious than ones that are owned, a Rolls Royce carries more prestige than a Cadillac, and nothing equals a Mercedes with the chrome painted black and the rear windows tinted to make the occupant invisible."[27]

They used to say you could judge a businessperson's seniority by the number of telephones on his or her desk. Today, as technology takes an ever firmer hold on business communications, business leaders find themselves increasingly dependent on IT specialists. Korda correctly states, "The first sign of a rise to power is often creeping helplessness."

Even shoes can symbolize power.

The influential leader will receive power as a gift and responsibility, not as a craved reward.

"Powerful people generally wear simple shoes," Korda says. "Five-eyelet shoes from Brooks Brothers, for example, and always put the laces in straight, not crisscrossed, and use round, waxed shoelaces. Shoes that have square toes, or high heels, or large brass buckles, or stitching in odd places, or are cut like jodhpur boots, are all definitely not power symbols, and to be avoided."[28]

Another power play involves the use of phones. Korda says, for instance, that receiving telephone calls diminishes power, while placing calls augments it. The ambitious executive, therefore, should do whatever is necessary to avoid taking calls. Far better to take messages and call back.

All this does not mean that an influential leader must reject the benefits of promotion, steadfastly refusing a salary increase, a personal assistant, or a larger office. In business, however, the trappings of power rarely disappear entirely. Symbolic endorsement of seniority can help you form and maintain relationships with important clients.

For example, a friend was once promoted from department head to vice president of a large publishing house and received some perks appropriate to his new position: invitations to high-level meetings, a company car, a new parking place, a new title. He attached little importance to such things, but he soon discovered that they meant a lot to the people who worked for him. The honor conferred on him reflected on his department, increasing commitment and morale.

Power does not bestow leadership;
personal authority does.

Leaders will possess some degree of power whether or not they seek it. For a group to recognize you as leader—even informally—bestows power. But the influential leader will receive power as a gift and responsibility, not as a craved reward. Power does not bestow leadership; personal authority does.

Visionary Decisions to Help You Lead with Effortless Grace

Leaders who do their job with effortless grace possess an authority that never stoops to coercion. Instead, they work by winning respect and trust. As with other aspects of influential leadership, this authority exists to some degree in everyone. You can nurture it and develop it. So resolve to make these visionary decisions to help you lead with effortless grace.

1. Lead with grace by accepting authority from others

I do not believe that anyone should exercise leadership over others until he or she has first learned to accept authority from another person.

Moreover, even when a person occupies a position of leadership, he or she should remain accountable to others. As leader, you may be accountable to others, such as your line manager or a personal mentor. Or you may be accountable to a group, such as a board of directors or trustees. In some situations, business leaders form accountability groups in which the group members make themselves accountable to one another.

> *Without accountability, even the best-intentioned person is open to the misuse of power.*

Influential leaders seek and respect accountability. Without it, even the best-intentioned person is open to the misuse of power.

2. Lead with grace by discovering yourself

Authority begins with self-knowledge. You must know who you are, and you must be happy with what you know.

Do you know yourself? Many try to keep their deepest desires, fears, and motivations a secret even from themselves. They close and lock the door on their inner psyche. Instead, they affect bravado, afraid that revealing their true selves will lead to rejection and failure.

The influential leader does not try to be somebody else. You can have true inner authority only if you are at peace with your inner self—if you understand that you are a person worth following. To reach that point, you must first discover yourself.

Spend time at the end of each day reflecting on what you have done and what you have learned about yourself. Step outside the circle of your self-interest and see yourself clearly and objectively. Write down your strengths and weaknesses.

> *Doing an inventory of your God-given qualities will keep your feet on the ground.*

Doing an inventory of your God-given qualities will keep your feet on the ground. You will know who you are. You will know that God accepts you and commissions you. And consequently you will enjoy far greater clarity in your relationships.

It would never dawn on an influential leader to seek a testimonial dinner in his honor. He has a sincere self-belief that arises through understanding, forgiving, and accepting himself. As an influential leader, you will neither desire the flattery of others nor feel the need to flatter. You will not look up to others or look down on them. You will neither seek compliments nor practice condescension.

The influential leader will always possess an inner strength. Though he may lack youth, health, and strength, his natural force will remain intact. He will remain calm and composed and never fear to look another person in the eye.

3. Lead with grace by developing self-confidence

You can release your self-confidence by eliminating the fear of failure.

Ironically, fear of failure often has little to do with failure itself. Rather it focuses on the consequences of failure—the prospect that your friends may abandon you or that you will suffer humiliation and shame.

You will overcome the fear of failure if you accept that this anxiety is irrational. Failure rarely leads to isolation or humiliation. Your friends will not condemn you for missing the mark, but they may question your judgment if you never even try. Good people never abandon the courageous, the honest, and the enterprising. They will admire your efforts. The greatest danger is not that they will abandon you but that you may abandon yourself.

Far better to attempt something great and fail than attempt nothing and succeed.

Far better to attempt something great and fail than attempt nothing and succeed.

Guilt also stifles self-confidence. Perhaps you have been programmed to feel guilty for having special gifts or power or skills. Those are gifts from God, and you should not feel guilty about them. Perhaps you feel you constantly fail to achieve God's high standards. Perhaps your personal appearance or a physical handicap bothers you. If you cannot change these things, accept them. Start by accepting yourself just as you are.

Next, compliment yourself. If you really accept yourself just as you are, you will find certain things about you that are worthy of gratitude. Each of us has negative traits and positive traits. Recognize those things out loud. Only after accepting yourself and complimenting yourself for your existing good points should you try to improve yourself.

Perhaps you should begin a program of vocabulary-building or a diet to lose weight or a careful plan for increasing your wealth. Whatever it is, your improvement will mean change for the better. And positive change means hope. Having a vision for change, planning the change, and seeing the change occur will develop your self-confidence, which in turn will strengthen your authority.

4. Lead with grace by accepting the importance of your vision

I observe many leaders completely immersed in their lifework, pursuing their mission with singleness of mind and purpose. These leaders tend to exhibit a greater authority than others. They know where they are going, and they direct those around them in a clear and focused way. Committed to people, projects, and an overriding cause, they think about ongoing responsibilities. All of this reinforces the confidence and competence that lies behind authority.

> *Leading with effortless grace requires that a leader pay attention to relationships.*

Without a strong vision, you will end up going over the same decisions again and again because you are constantly of two minds and tempted to change direction. In that state, everything is negotiable, even the vision you claim to pursue. You will always be looking for some new fad or activity that will get the attention of the public.

5. Lead with grace by remembering your relationship with others

Leading with effortless grace requires that a leader pay attention to relationships. Conduct matters. So too does the impression you make. For example:

- *Don't reveal fatigue.* If you are committed to a goal and you enjoy working toward that goal, you can sometimes overlook the warning signs of fatigue. In many cases, others will notice your tiredness before you do, and this damages their confidence in you. When you are tired, admit it to yourself and get out of public view. Get your rest. Let people see you only when you are vigorous. You may be the boss, the page-one celebrity, the top athlete, but the moment others see you fatigued, they see weakness, and their trust can erode.

- *Keep your own counsel.* Sharing your joys and woes, talking about your achievements and setbacks, finding a sympathetic ear—all these give comfort. But, except in some special relationships, this action will dilute your authority. The American statesman and scientist Benjamin Franklin said, "Let no man know thee thoroughly; men freely ford that see the shallows." This does not mean you should be furtive or devious. It simply means that you should have a degree of self-sufficiency. Limit your self-disclosure to a few trusted people—your husband or wife, a close friend or mentor. Otherwise, keep your thoughts to yourself.

- *Respect the rights and emotions of others.* Let people know you are aware of them. Be sensitive to their individuality, their achievements, their position. Give honor to whom honor is due, but don't do it obsequiously. Show regard for the concepts, the intelligence, and the abilities of others. Don't tell the carpenter how to do his work nor the doctor how to diagnose your physical condition. Use good manners; practice courtesy. Show as much respect for the person who answers the telephone in an office as you do for the president of the company. Show knowledge of—and concern for—the culture of another person. Accommodate other people's beliefs and customs unless they produce a serious conflict with your values. Respect others, and in so doing you will avoid rudeness or criticism or inconsiderateness.

6. Lead with grace by striving for excellence

In everything, do the best you can. Excellence brings its own satisfaction, and doing your best will reinforce your authority in the eyes of your followers.

Excellence brings its own satisfaction.

Everyone can excel in some area. Look again at those areas of strength you found when you discovered yourself. Those are the areas you should concentrate on in your striving for excellence, because those are the places where you can most naturally excel.

Summary

When we say that somebody is a natural leader, we usually mean that he or she possesses authority. Authority resides in a variety of things—charisma, track record, self-esteem, personality—that collectively command the respect of others.

Authority has nothing to do with a person's physical characteristics or actions. Nor does it depend on wealth, social position, or status. You do not need success in order to acquire it. Authority lies in the conviction that you can move the people in your group toward goals of beneficial permanence.

Many confuse authority with power. But power has no roots in personal strength and ability. A person acquires power from others, and they can take it back. In business, particularly, the signs and trappings of power confer advantages. First, they act as signals that you have attained a certain level of seniority. And second, they can sometimes reflect well on and symbolize the success of the team working under you.

But seeking power for its own sake will distract you from your vision. If you become focused on boosting your social status or rely on power as a means of influencing and motivating others, you are unlikely to progress far with leadership. Having too much interest in being the boss impairs the authority on which all leadership success depends. If your followers do not respect you for who you are, you can never truly lead them.

STEP 12

DECIDE TO THRIVE ON AMBIGUITY

I mentioned earlier the trip I made to Beirut in 1964. Then the days of solitude I spent on Indonesia's island of Bali hammering out the vision for advanced international leadership training.

At first I had no plans to implement the vision myself. My son, a quadriplegic, loved me and I adored him. God had given him a great mind, but a Quasimodo body trapped his outstanding mental capabilities. Because of his needs, I had no intention of traveling.

So I took the vision to my denomination, thinking they would immediately grasp the concept and adopt it as a world missions strategy. What could make more sense than training Christian leaders from developing countries? Being born in their respective cultures, these leaders would relate far better to their fellow nationals than would Western missionaries. And the cost of keeping one missionary in the field for 20 years would provide training for 200 credentialed national leaders.

A moment's historical analysis reveals that influence starts at the top, never at the bottom. Is that not true in the establishment of a church or the launching of a business or the founding of a school?

Therefore, strategic missions thinking zeroes in on those with top positions and impeccable credentials. Even if I were the greatest orator since Demosthenes and the greatest strategist since Joshua, how could I begin to impact the multiple millions of people that these stellar leaders would reach? It seemed self-evident.

But my denominational leaders rejected the idea. They scoffed at it. In their view, decision making belonged with them. They required the leaders of the national ministries to move in lockstep with the international headquarters based in the United States.

In fact, though, most of those heading up the home office had not worked on the mission field for years. In that time, conditions had drastically changed. For instance, at the end of World War II, Asia could point to only two sovereign nations: Japan and Thailand. Western powers stood in colonial oversight of every other nation on the world's largest continent.

Now, less than 20 years later, each was a sovereign nation. That changed the mindset. Will free and independent people submit to the edicts of those who look upon them as subordinate or inferior? You know the answer.

I need to say that the heads of my denomination's mission board later visited me to apologize for "30 years of obstruction." Of course their hearts were right. It was my view then, as it is my view now, that they lacked essential information and perspective.

---

*Nothing so devastates progress
in world evangelism as Westerners who
sincerely believe that God has given them a
mandate to impose their agenda on others.*

But nothing so devastates progress in world evangelism as Westerners—particularly Westerners who are willing to die for Christ—who sincerely believe that God has given them a mandate to impose their Western agenda on others.

Some of my dearest friends criticized me, saying, "How can John

Haggai, a second-generation product of foreign missions, undermine the glorious ministry of our foreign missionaries?"

Nobody got it. Many still don't get it, even after four decades in which border after border has closed to missionaries. A generation has passed, and the same mindset still grips the thinking of Western churches. Even if they accept the model of training non-Western leaders to evangelize, they still insist that the West must conduct the training.

The issue here is ambiguity. Geopolitical patterns shift subtly almost daily. If, indeed, history ever did record a day of fixed realities, of certainty, of stability, that day vanished long ago. The themes today are uncertainty, change, contradiction. Holding onto the methods of 100 years ago may offer psychological comfort, but it will not make your leadership relevant, influential, or effective.

Leaders have to thrive on ambiguity.

Ambiguity on the Ground

A static situation, where little changes and everything moves forward on a more or less predictable path, does not call for leadership, only management.

Throw in uncertainty—the likelihood that today's success may turn into tomorrow's failure, that today's safety may turn into tomorrow's jeopardy—and you suddenly need leaders. If leaders can't handle ambiguity—can't anticipate it, can't ride it—they are not providing leadership.

If I cannot tolerate uncertainty, I will want to go to great lengths to resolve it. Unfortunately, in most leadership situations time constraints preclude such action. Further, the necessary information may stay beyond my reach even if I have time to look for it.

The influential leader recognizes the need to take risks and practices clear decision making.

This forces me to leap in the dark. In such a situation a person who cannot face uncertainty either dithers in indecision or collapses under the strain. In contrast, the influential leader recognizes the need to take risks and practices clear decision making—not the same thing, by the way, as simply gambling or being too lazy to study the available data.

But ambiguity deals with uncertainty not only in decision making but also in knowledge. Can I have certainty in my knowledge of God? No. I apprehend God only by faith. My belief in God makes a faith statement rather than a scientific statement.

Many friends waste time trying to prove that belief in God is rational. I find it incredible that people should do so. All statements, even those of science, are ultimately based on faith—that is, on assumptions no one can independently verify. For instance, one must always assume a first cause no matter what the philosophy or theology.

What distinguishes the influential leader derives from his ability to live by a statement of faith rather than by the appearance of circumstances around him. A person who cannot face ambiguity cannot do this. In the end, any vision expresses a statement of faith. Man can never have a certainty of tomorrow. He believes God revealed the vision. That gives him faith in the vision and motivates him to take the necessary action to realize it.

All influential leaders take risks and commit their
lives entirely to the vision.

That explains why all influential leaders take risks and commit their lives entirely to the vision. They see a future reality, where others prefer to live in the certainty of the present and the certain guidance of their superiors.

But ambiguity exists not only in my life purpose and goal. Ambiguity also pervades daily life. A person who cannot stand ambiguity makes for himself a code of rules or laws to tell him what to do in every situation. By this he avoids having to take responsibility for what he does. He simply obeys instructions.

An influential leader never hesitates to take responsibility for his actions. He does not look at the rules but at the value system behind the rules. He makes visionary decisions based on the interaction between his value system and his current situation.

This can lead to much uncertainty, especially where values clash. But the influential leader lives with the risk of a wrong decision. He knows that the worst decision is no decision. He further knows he should not aim to make right decisions but to make decisions right. The first implies that every decision either conforms, or fails to conform, to a perfect, preordained divine plan. The second, reflecting James 1:5, simply urges us to decide responsibly on the basis of such wisdom as we receive from God.

That's why I avoid implicating God in my decision making. No one has ever heard me say, "The Lord has led me to do such and such." If the endeavor demonstrates the movement of His mighty hand, I then say, "The Lord led in this matter."

When I studied for the ministry, a fellow student said, "The Lord has led Susie and me to get married." A few months later, when I inquired about the state of their romance, he said, "The Lord led us to break off the engagement."

"The Lord is having a hard time making up His mind about you, isn't He?" I said.

I determined that I would not presume upon the specifics of God's leadership. Neither would I budge without my strong sense that He was leading in a given matter.

When you refuse to make your own decisions,
someone else makes the decisions for you.

When you refuse to make your own decisions, someone else makes the decisions for you. As a result, you lose your freedom and become a slave to someone else. In Galatians 3 and 4, Paul talks about bondage to the law in contrast to a state of spiritual maturity where you experience freedom from the law and take responsibility for yourself.

Influential leaders live a life of faith and trust in God. They abandon forever the need for certainty about where they will end up in this life. As the author of Hebrews says, Abraham did not know where he was going. But he knew by faith the God who was taking him there.

Don't Expect Ambiguity to Diminish

In the early years, I had no certainty that the Haggai Institute concept would work.

For 22 years I lived on the brink of personal financial disaster. Only one time in 17 years was money available for a training seminar on the day the seminar began.

Those skilled in dealing with ambiguity frustrate others by not getting specific enough or by not being detailed in an orderly handling of problem solving. In the 1960s, I acted on the vision that I believed God had given me. I did not have a lot of the answers. Yet an overseas leader, whose intelligence and position I admire and respect, told me recently that Haggai Institute has greater influence today than the foreign ministry department of any nation.

Forty years ago the challenge was survival. At that time, Haggai Institute had no money, no prestige, and no track record. Now, with millions of dollars in assets, a track record recognized globally, and an opportunity of unprecedented proportions, the challenge focuses on keeping the organization true to the vision on which it was founded. And that requires taking risks within an increasingly ambiguous geopolitical environment.

---

*The men and women who have
made the world great had
no safety net to catch them.*

Very often, the men and women who have made the world great had no safety net to catch them.

I think of John Templeton who changed twentieth-century investing concepts by introducing global investing.

I think of Richard M. DeVos and his colleague Jay Van Andel. They took enormous risks and they paid heavy prices. Today, people see only the financial value of the business.

I think of Mochtar Riady and his sons, James and Stephen. Mochtar took the risk of launching into business. He built world-class "Cities of Tomorrow" and never borrowed money in order to do it.

James told me that his father visited the proposed city location and convinced the Indonesians living in shacks along the highway to trust him and to work for him. He provided them with good housing and an economic lifestyle greater than they could have envisioned.

---

*"Nothing will ever be attempted if all possible
obstacles must first be overcome."*

True, today Mochtar and his sons are super-wealthy. But that follows years during which they lived and worked with considerable ambiguity. And in today's global environment, ambiguity remains a fact of life at every economic level.

I keep a plaque in my office that says: *Nothing will ever be attempted if all possible obstacles must first be overcome.* People who can't tolerate ambiguity must have all the answers before they make a move. They never attain their potential.

Are You Ambiguity Tolerant?

Those who thrive on ambiguity will work comfortably with change. As the Greek philosopher Heraclitus put it, "You cannot step in the same river twice." Things may look the same, but they never are. Constant change permeates all existence. The present becomes the past, the future becomes the present.

Change happens constantly. All living things have within them a natural tendency to grow. Look at a tree and you see, visually mapped out, the history of that organism's struggle to develop against the resisting forces of gravity and wind. You will never see a static tree. Nor can any organization remain static.

Change does not wait for you any more than a moving car waits for the driver to take a grip on the wheel. The car is already in motion. That means that societies and companies and organizations will, in an almost literal way, crash unless the person in leadership has the ability to negotiate change. It's about reading the road and using the steering.

> *A leader must not simply tolerate or accept change, but actually encourage it.*

John Templeton once told me that "a leader must encourage change." He must not simply tolerate or accept it, but actually *encourage* it. At the time, Templeton was 70 years old. I found it refreshing to spend time with a person who took a proactive stance with his business and who used the past only to give insight into the present and direction for planning the future.

In their program, the Ambiguity Architect, Randall P. White and Philip Hodgson[29] identify the behaviors of those skilled and unskilled in ambiguity. Those skilled in dealing with ambiguity:

- Can effectively cope with change

- Can shift gears comfortably without need of detailed explanation
- Can decide and act without having the total picture
- Aren't stressed when things are up in the air
- Don't have to finish tasks before moving on
- Can comfortably handle risk and uncertainty

By contrast, those unskilled in ambiguity:

- Are not comfortable with change or uncertainty
- May not do well on fuzzy problems with no clear solution or outcome
- May prefer more data than others and structure over uncertainty
- Prefer things tacked down and sure
- Are less efficient and productive under ambiguity
- Are too quick to close
- May have a strong need to finish everything
- May like to do things the same way time after time

The question is one of fit. People who dislike ambiguity play a vital part in organizations. They lean toward defined, detailed, and measurable activities. They perform well on reports, numbers, and intricate responsibilities. All organizations need those abilities.

But only those who thrive on ambiguity can start at ground zero and accomplish great things. Those are the people who have learned influential leadership. They have made visionary decisions to lead rather than maintain.

Visionary Decisions to Help You Thrive on Ambiguity

Without managers, leaders cannot set up the organizational structure to pursue and maintain a vision. But without leaders, managers have nothing to manage. You will never escape ambiguity. Influential leaders learn to turn ambiguity to their advantage. So resolve to make these visionary decisions to help you thrive on ambiguity.

1. Thrive on ambiguity by determining your next move now

It's mandatory to determine in advance your next move.

If you wait until your previous move has been fulfilled, then you'll find yourself drifting in the wasteland of unnecessary uncertainty. In the normal course of a day, you will feel at times that the situation is opaque. It's like looking through a frosted glass and trying to see inside the room. Actions, reactions, and unexpected developments can smudge your plan of action.

*Do your strategic thinking
before you reach the crisis.*

So do your strategic thinking before you reach the crisis. Once in the crisis, too many things will compete for your attention. You will find it more difficult to act decisively and in a way that moves you toward your goal.

2. Thrive on ambiguity by keeping your eyes on your destination

When God laid upon my heart the vision to bring the Gospel to everyone on the planet in culturally relevant terms—terms they would understand—I had no idea how events would actually play out. Situations arose that nearly derailed the process.

I've already referred to the reception I got from my denominational mission board. In some ways even more challenging was hearing my father, for whom I had and still have inexpressible respect, urge me to stay in the pastorate.

"John, God has given you such an outstanding pulpit ministry," he said. "You're preaching to thousands. Why are you now moving into another area of service?"

That was a tough moment.

But unless you refer back to your vision and detailed plan for achieving what you aim for, you will become a slave to the immediate environment and temporal situations that may lack long-term significance. You will feel helpless if you constantly allow the immediate environment to determine your actions.

The celebrated Indian derivatives trader Ashwani Gujral always insists on reading three different chart levels—monthly data, end of day data, and hourly data. Knowing the trend at the higher levels, he insists, will prevent you entering an adverse trade at a lower level, even if the lowest-level chart seems to present an alluring opportunity.[30]

Visionary decision making follows much the same pattern. You may not always identify a direction in day-to-day, hour-to-hour events. Confusing or distracting events may intervene. Some of these can hit you very hard. They may undermine your confidence at precisely the moment those around you need strength and security.

You must make things clear
to the people who follow you
so they will not be frightened to
follow you to the destination.

The people who follow you don't always see the bigger picture. Therefore, you must make things as detailed and clear to them as possible so they will not be frightened to follow you to the destination. You'll find it perfectly uplifting and energizing to tell them the destination while you yourself have written down in detail the intermediate steps to that destination.

3. Thrive on ambiguity by cultivating your awareness

During the Army-McCarthy hearings in the 1950s, Ray Jenkins, a lawyer from Tennessee, was summoned to Washington to represent Senator Joseph McCarthy and his group. His fairness in the proceedings was attested by the manner in which he was assailed by partisans of both sides.

McCarthy did not impress me. But I was so impressed with Jenkins that in 1956 I phoned him to ask if I could visit him at his office in Knoxville. I was 32 years of age, and I wanted to learn from him.

I had done my homework and discovered that he was considered one of the most successful lawyers in America during the middle part of the last century. In conversation he said that his success stemmed from three things: first, from his refusal to take any case in which he did not passionately believe; second, from the fact that he could remember every word of testimony from each witness; and third, from his ability to recall not only the words but the emotional bias of the witnesses.

At that point he turned to me and said, "You look a little quizzical."

I apologized, but had to admit I found his claims hard to believe.

"You question my memory?"

"Well, you have to admit it's unusual for a man to do what you say you can do," I said.

"I know the telephone number of every lawyer in the state of Tennessee," he said. "Do you know a lawyer in Tennessee?"

I told him I did.

"OK, tell me his name."

I gave him the name of one of the least-known country lawyers, who lived in a remote town more than 500 miles (800 kilometers) away.

He said to me, "Do you want his home phone number or his office number?"

"Well, just find him wherever you can."

Without referring to any list, the man dialed and got the country lawyer on the phone.

I was amazed.

We spent a couple of hours talking. He was one of the most accomplished individuals I have ever met. Nothing escaped his observation.

I have known leaders like that in other parts of the world. Another man who astounded me with his ability to recall detailed information was a Swiss industrialist by the name of Jean André of Lausanne. His keenness of mind and lightning-quick recall put him ahead of the competition in negotiations.

An influential leader remains constantly aware of what happens around him and constantly aware of the context. Both the ability to see problems coming and the ability to act quickly and decisively depend on being able to fit current events into the background pattern of events stored in memory.

Awareness can be learned and improved.

My mother gave birth to three baby boys in four years. This was in a day before labor-saving devices. We had no inside plumbing. Mother did not have an electric iron, an automatic dishwasher, a washing machine or dryer, or a refrigerator. Not even an icebox.

This frail woman of poor health worked tirelessly and uncomplainingly to take care of the needs of her husband and the three babies.

Dad inculcated in me an awareness
of my surroundings for which I still thank him,
many years after his death.

I was the oldest, and my father would keep me with him a great deal of the time to take some of the pressure off my mother. Dad inculcated in me an awareness of my surroundings for which I still thank him, many years after his death. We would drive past a billboard and he would say to me (then four years old), "John Edmund, what was on that billboard?"

Coming back from a church meeting he would ask, "What color

hat was the lady who sat on the platform wearing? What was the third point of my sermon? In what kind of car did Mr. Beneway drive away from church?"

I remember how frustrated I would become at this nonstop plying of questions. But what a debt I owe to my father. Today, very little escapes my observation. The discipline that he instilled in me has increased my awareness and trained my memory. If I had grandchildren today, I would do the same thing with them because I have learned the value of it.

I cannot overemphasize the power of good recall.
Awareness produces excellence.

Not everybody will have that experience. However, the leader can advance his effectiveness if he disciplines himself to recall his recent experiences. For example:

- What color tie did the vice president wear this morning?
- How many chairs circled the conference table?
- What pictures did the CEO of the company have on the walls?
- What airline was an associate scheduled to take to Paris this afternoon?

I cannot overemphasize the power of good recall. Awareness produces excellence. This is true not only of leaders but of athletes, musicians, orators, businesspeople, dancers, and writers. This proves true in every area of life. To excel, a person must understand what contributes to excellence and constantly measure his performance against set standards.

4. Thrive on ambiguity by attempting something so great for God it's doomed to fail unless God is in it

In the pursuit of my God-given vision, I incurred not only the misunderstanding and even the antagonism of some of my best friends, but also a huge financial cost. I lost my entire estate. By the mercy of God I was able to keep my home. But I cashed in my insurance policies. I decimated my savings. My income took a severe hit. From being the highest-paid clergyman on American soil, I was reduced to $1350 a month. My invalid son was costing $10,000 to $11,000 a year.

I told no one. How God kept us together constitutes, in my thinking, a miracle. I did not emerge from debt for 22 years. People who know me will attest that I am a prudent and careful money manager. The Internal Revenue Service went over my books 11 times in 19 years. Every time it was "NC"—no change. They just could not bring themselves to believe that anybody would give as large a percentage of income to charitable organizations as I did.

When the last one of the IRS leaders met with me, he said, "Come on, Dr. Haggai, suppose the situation were reversed. What would you think?"

"I would think that you believed the Bible just as much as I do!" I said.

"My son is studying at the Presbyterian Seminary for the ministry," he said. "I wish you would talk to him."

I chuckled. "It is not he who needs the talk; it is you."

Over the course of 30 years I lost at least three of the finest executives I have ever known. They gave or raised thousands of dollars for the ministry. They believed in the Haggai Institute vision. They just came to the conclusion it was doomed to fail. One of them told me to my face that we should dissolve the ministry and give the assets to another Christian organization.

*If you don't need God's help,
then you probably lack ambition.*

Was I discouraged? No, because in saying the task was impossible, that man also affirmed my vision. If you don't need God's help, then you probably lack ambition.

If I had caved amid the concerns of others—if I had shared their fears—the ministry would not exist today. Millions upon millions who have heard the Gospel through the laymen and clergy trained at Haggai Institute would never have heard it.

Not long ago, one of the world's great financiers took the training at our Maui center. He was 48 years of age and planned to retire at 50. God so spoke to him during that training session that today, at 53, he is more active than before. He has been a major force in building, in the Arab-speaking world, a church building and staff that would do credit to any Christian organization in the West.

Summary

Influential leadership results from visionary decision making. Visionary decisions—small decisions as well as great—are decisions consistent with the overall direction of your life, ministry, and work.

No contradiction should exist in a leader's life, though he may well need to choose priorities. However, there will always be ambiguity. Leadership, which I define as *the discipline of deliberately exerting special influence within a group to move it toward goals of beneficial permanence that fulfill the group's real needs,* forces the leader to make decisions with imperfect information.

Influential leaders do not avoid ambiguity; rather they seek to thrive on it.

Influential leaders do not avoid ambiguity; rather they seek to thrive on it. To have a vision, after all, means you take a position of faith about the future. You do not know what will happen. You do know very clearly what you believe you are called to do, and you take responsibility for visionary decision making that moves you toward your ultimate objective.

Ambiguity never goes away. It just changes shape. As an influential leader you stand between that ambiguity and the people you lead. You can take visionary decisions that help you thrive on ambiguity by using forethought, by keeping focused on your destination, and by cultivating your awareness.

Many authorities on management will tell you to diminish ambiguity and increase certainty. Actually you need to do the opposite. Ambiguity belongs right at the center of change. And it belongs at the heart of your vision. If you make the visionary decision to "do something so great for God that it's doomed to fail unless God is in it," you are embracing ambiguity as a sailing ship embraces the wind.

The world has never been in greater need of influential leaders. Without doubt, you have the potential to become one. The fact you have read through this book convinces me of that. You can close the book and put it back on the shelf. Or you can start on a life-transforming journey of leadership.

Either way, it's a visionary decision.

NOTES

1. W.C.H. Prentice, "Understanding Leadership," *Harvard Business Review,* No. 61511, September-October 1961, quoted in *Paths Toward Personal Progress: Leaders Are Made, Not Born* (Boston: Harvard Business Review, 1980), 1.

2. *Harvard Business Review,* September-October 1961; reprinted as the lead article in the collection *Paths Toward Personal Progress: Leaders are Made, Not Born* (Boston: Harvard Business Review, 1982).

3. Quoted in Stephen B. Oates, *Let the Trumpet Sound: The Life of Martin Luther King Jr.* (New York: Harper and Row, 1982), 260-61.

4. Harvard International Monitoring Group (HMAG), *Lee Kuan Yew* (HMAG Profile No. 2), 1.

5. See Michael Rozek, "Mr. Write," in *Success Magazine,* March 1984.

6. Ibid.

7. Peter J. Daniels, *How to Be Happy Though Rich* (Unley Park, South Australia: The House of Taylor, 1984), 113-23.

8. Ari Kiev, *A Strategy for Daily Living* (New York: Free Press, 1973), 2-3, 30.

9. O. Carl Simonton, Stephanie Matthew-Simonton, and James L. Creighton, *Getting Well Again* (New York: Bantam Books, 1978), 97, 173-84.

10. Harold Geneen, *Managing* (Garden City, NY: Doubleday, 1984), reprinted in *Best of Business,* vol. 6, 6.

11. William Funk and Norman Lewis, *Thirty Days to a More Powerful Vocabulary,* rev. ed. by Norman Lewis (Garden City, NY: Doubleday, 1984).

12. Geneen, *Managing,* 14.

13. Denis Waitley, *Seeds of Greatness* (Old Tappan, NJ: Fleming H. Revell, 1983), 27-28.

14. Ted W. Engstrom with Robert C. Larson, *The Fine Art of Friendship* (Nashville: Thomas Nelson Publishers, 1985).

15. Erich Fromm, *The Art of Loving* (New York: Bantam Books, 1956), 90-92.

16. Richard Foster, *Celebration of Discipline* (San Francisco: Harper and Row, 1978), 5.

17. Proverbs 16:32.

18. As reported by Les Giblin, *How to Have Confidence and Power in Dealing with People*

(Englewood Cliffs, NJ: Prentice-Hall, 1956), 107. See Alvin C. Busse and Richard C. Borden, *How to Win an Argument* (1926; repr., Whitefish, MT: Kessinger Publishing, 2003).

19. Herschel H. Hobbs, *Who Is This?* (Nashville: Broadman Press, 1952), 53.

20. Andrew Tanzer, "The Amazing Mr. Kuok," *Forbes,* 28 July 1997, 91.

21. Thomas J. Peters and Robert H. Waterman Jr., *In Search of Excellence* (San Francisco: Harper and Row, 1982), 164-65.

22. Kenneth H. Cooper, *The Aerobics Program for Total Well Being* (New York: M. Evans and Company, 1982).

23. Nathan Pritikin with Patrick M. McGrady Jr., *The Pritikin Program for Diet and Exercise* (New York: Bantam Books, 1980), xx.

24. Marie Beynon Rae, *How Never to Be Tired* (New York: Bobbs-Merrill Company, 1954).

25. William Golding, *Lord of the Flies* (New York: Capricorn Books, 1954), 19.

26. Ida Tarbell, *The History of the Standard Oil Company* (Gloucester, MA: Peter Smith Publisher, 1963), 105-6.

27. Michael Korda, *Power: How to Get It, How to Use It* (New York: Ballantine Books, 1975), 219.

28. Ibid., 209-10.

29. See http://www.edgp.com/positive_change.html

30. Ashwani Gujral, *How to Make Money Trading Derivatives* (New Delhi: Vision Books, 2005), ch. 4.

RECOMMENDED READING

Over the years I have gained many insights from academics and speakers. But I find myself drawn toward the leaders who have personally created an enterprise and understand leadership from the inside. On that basis a handful of writers deserve special mention.

Rich DeVos has blazed a trail with his innovative and highly successful leadership style. He remains, in my view, one of America's superlative practitioners in business.

Anthony D'Souza possesses one of the most astute business minds I have ever encountered. A Jesuit, he has founded two outstanding management institutes and remains head of the Xavier Institute of Management in Mumbai, India.

James MacGregor Burns, Pulitzer Prize winner and Woodrow Wilson Professor (emeritus) of Political Science at Williams College, has served as president of two major research organizations as well as writing the groundbreaking book *Transforming Leadership*.

John Maxwell has been a pastor as well as a lecturer and writer. While not seminal, his highly popular books on leadership reveal a masterly skill at codifying and presenting the elements of good leadership.

Finally, *Michael Youssef,* author of the influential *Leadership Style of Jesus,* started his Atlanta church with fewer than 40 adults. Multiple thousands now attend. His Church of the Apostles has just built a $70 million facility debt-free. That shows some extraordinary leadership.

Bennis, Warren, and Burt Nanus. *Leaders: The Strategies for Taking Charge.* New York: Harper and Row, 1985.

Bogardus, Henry S. *Leaders and Leadership.* New York: Appleton-Century-Crofts, 1934.

Burns, John McGregor. *Transforming Leadership: A New Pursuit of Happiness.* New York: Atlantic Monthly Press, 2003.

Cooper, Kenneth H. *The Aerobics Program for Total Well Being.* New York: M. Evans and Company, 1982.

Daniels, Peter J. *How to Be Happy Though Rich.* Unley Park, South Australia: House of Taylor, 1984.

DeVos, Rich. *Compassionate Capitalism: People Helping People Help Themselves.* New York: Penguin, 1993.

———. *Ten Powerful Phrases for Positive People.* New York: Center Street, 2008.

Drucker, Peter F. *The Effective Executive.* New York: Harper and Row Publishers, 1966.

D'Souza, Anthony. *Leaders for Today, Hope for Tomorrow: Empowering and Empowered Leadership.* Mumbai: Pauline Publications, 2003.

Edersheim, Alfred. *The Life and Times of Jesus the Messiah.* Grand Rapids, MI: Wm. B. Eerdmans Publishing Company, 1947.

Engstrom, Ted W. *The Making of a Christian Leader.* Grand Rapids, MI: Zondervan Publishing House, 1976.

Eubank and Auer. *Discussion and Debate.* New York: F. S. Crofts and Company, 1946.

Forbes, B. *America's Twelve Master Salesmen.* New York: Forbes and Sons Publishing Company, 1952.

Forbes, Rosalind. *Corporate Stress.* Garden City, NY: Doubleday and Company, 1979.

Geneen, Harold. *Managing.* Garden City, NY: Doubleday and Company, 1984.

Gujral, Ashwani. *How to Make Money Trading Derivatives.* New Delhi: Vision Books, 2005.

Haggai, John Edmund. *How to Win Over Worry.* Updated ed. Eugene, OR: Harvest House Publishers, 2001.

———. *The Seven Secrets of Successful Business Relationships.* London: HarperCollins, 1999.

Harvey, Paul. *The Rest of the Story.* Compiled by Lynne Harvey. Chicago: Paulynne, 1969.

Iacocca, Lee. *Iacocca: An Autobiography.* New York: Bantam Books, 1984.

Josey, Alex. *Lee Kuan Yew: The Struggle for Singapore.* London: Angus and Robertson Publishers, 1976.

Kiev, Ari. *A Strategy for Daily Living.* New York: Free Press, 1973.

Lowney, Chris. *Heroic Leadership: Best Practices from a 450-Year-Old Company that Changed the World.* Chicago: Loyola University Press, 2005.

Matthews, Basil. *John R. Mott, World Citizen.* New York: Harper and Brothers, 1934.

Maxwell, John. *The 21 Irrefutable Laws of Leadership: Follow Them and People Will Follow You.* Nashville: Thomas Nelson Publishers, 1998.

McCormack, Mark H. *What They Don't Teach You at Harvard Business School.* New York: Bantam Books, 1984.

Meyer, Paul J. *Dynamics of Goal Setting.* Waco, TX: Success Motivation Institute, 1977.

————. *Dynamics of Personal Motivation.* 3rd ed. Waco, TX: Success Motivation Institute, 1983.

Montgomery, Field-Marshal. *Path to Leadership.* New York: G. T. Putnam and Sons, 1961.

Nixon, Richard. *Leaders.* New York: Warner Books, 1982.

Ogilvy, David. *On Advertising.* New York: Vintage Books, 1985.

Phillips, Arthur Edward. *Effective Speaking.* Chicago: Newton Company, 1922.

Ryle, J.C. *Christian Leaders of the Eighteenth Century.* Edinburgh: Banner of Truth Trust, 1885.

Sadat, Anwar. *Sadat: An Autobiography.* London: Fontana/Collins, 1978.

Sandburg, Carl. *Abraham Lincoln: The Prairie Years and the War Years.* New York: Harcourt Brace, 1954.

Scammell, Michael. *Solzhenitsyn.* New York: W. W. Norton and Company, 1985.

Seabury, David. *How to Get Things Done.* Garden City, NY: Halcyon House, 1938.

Spurgeon, Charles Haddon. *C. H. Spurgeon's Autobiography.* 4 vols. London: Passmore and Alabaster, 1899-1900.

Taylor, Robert Lewis. *Winston Churchill.* New York: Pocket Books, 1952.

Templeton, John M. *The Humble Approach: Scientists Discover God.* New York: Seabury Press, 1981.

Tzu, Sun. *The Art of War.* Translated by Samuel B. Griffith. London: Oxford University Press, 1963.

Weber, Max. *On Charisma and Institution Building.* Chicago: University of Chicago Press, 1968.

Wesley, John. *The Journal of John Wesley.* 8 vols. London: Epworth Press, 1938.

Youssef, Michael. *The Leadership Style of Jesus.* Wheaton, IL: Victor Books, 1986.

INDEX

About the Author

John Edmund Haggai has spent a lifetime studying and teaching leadership.

In 65 years of public service, he has pastored four churches, held evangelistic campaigns around the world, and established an advanced leadership training program with more than 75,000 alumni in 182 countries. Truly a world Christian statesman, he has crisscrossed six continents, circled the globe 103 times, and met numerous heads of state.

He was born in Louisville, Kentucky, son of a Syrian immigrant and a New Englander whose English ancestors settled in America during the 1600s. An alumnus of both Moody Bible Institute and Furman University, Haggai was named "Alumnus of the Year" by Moody and has received honorary doctorates on both sides of the Pacific.

His audiences have ranged from British parliamentarians to People's Republic of China leaders, the Kiwanis International Convention, the Texas Medical Association, international investment bankers on Wall Street, graduate students at Yale University, an Anglican congregation in Singapore, and a symposium led by leaders of India's ten major religions.

Churches flourished under his leadership, and in 1954-55 his Baptist church registered more conversions and additions by baptism than any church in the leading 11 evangelical denominations of America. More than 400 invitations within an 18-month period affirmed God's call into fulltime evangelistic campaigns.

During his first trip to Asia in the 1960s, Dr. Haggai realized changes in global geopolitics—brought about by the end of colonialism—required new strategies for world evangelism. The need to mobilize nationals to reach their own people was clear. After much research, prayer, and development, the first advanced leadership seminar was conducted in 1969.

Despite extraordinary family demands (his son suffered from cerebral palsy), Dr. Haggai has established a unique international ministry and written numerous influential books. His first book, *How to Win Over Worry*, has sold millions of copies in 19 languages.

John Edmund Haggai and his wife, Christine, live in Atlanta, Georgia—their influence touches millions of people around the world.

For more information about Dr. Haggai or Haggai Institute, visit www.haggai-institute.com.

How to Win over Worry
Time-Tested Answers to Emotional Freedom

This classic bestseller on conquering worry (over 2 million copies in print in 32 languages) has a fresh, eye-catching cover and a new mass size!

For more than 45 years people have turned to John Edmund Haggai's *How to Win over Worry* for practical answers and solutions. Updated in 2001, its attractive new size and price will reach a fresh generation of readers with biblical truths that can set them free.

Real-life examples, revealing insights, and honest evaluation will show you the powerful tools God provides to break the bonds of anxiety and stress. Biblical answers are encapsulated in a proven formula—a new way of thinking that will help you win over worry...and begin enjoying the peace God promises.

John Edmund Haggai, founder and president of Haggai Institute, is an internationally acclaimed author, lecturer, and "leader of leaders." He has helped people around the world with his practical formulas for winning over worry, pain, loneliness, and "impossible" situations.